WYM

D1394685

RAILWAYS

AMAZING AND EXTRAORDINARY FACTS

RAILWAYS

Julian Holland

RYDON
PUBLISHING

A Rydon Publishing Book
35 The Quadrant
Hassocks
West Sussex
BN6 8BP
www.rydonpublishing.co.uk
www.rydonpublishing.com

Revised edition first published by Rydon Publishing in 2015
First published by David & Charles in 2007

A CIP catalogue record for this book is available from the British Library.

ISBN: 978-1-910821-00-8

Printed in Great Britain by Polestar Wheatons

CONTENTS

Introduction	7	120 Into 4 = The Big Four	70
Crash!	12	4 Into 1 = BR	74
A Local Train of Thought by		Narrow Gauge Adventure	76
Siegfried Sassoon	15	A Right Royal Railway	80
An Eccentric Railway Empire	16	The Dockers' Umbrella	82
To a Great Western Broad Gauge		The Streakers	84
Engine and its Stoker by		*King's Cross Station* by	
Horatio Brown	21	GK Chesterton	87
A Bridge Too Far	22	Mr Bradshaw – Friend of the	
How Rats Ruined a Railway	24	Railway Traveller	88
Birth and Death of a Railway	26	A Quick Snog in the Back Row	90
The Railway Junction by		What a Wind-up!	92
Walter de la Mare	29	Island Railways	94
Find Your Local Shed Code!	30	*The Send-off* by Wilfred Owen	101
Battle of the Gauges	34	A Railway Institution	102
Famous Locomotive Engineers	36	Once There Were Only Fields	104
From a Railway Carriage by Robert		Working for 'The Firm'	106
Louis Stevenson	37	What a Bore!	108
Famous Locomotive Engineers	38	From Gunboats to Corpses	110
Faster and Faster	42	Gee up!	112
British Rail Speed Records	43	Along Strange Lines	114
The Last Main Line	44	Cliffhangers	118
Famous Locomotive Designers	46	Smile Please!	120
Warships and Westerns	48	What's in a Name?	124
Dr Beeching, I Presume!	52	Gauging the Width	126
On Shed, 7th April 1963	54	King of the Castles	128
Fair Exchange	56	Welsh Phoenix	130
Small is Beautiful	60	No More Buckets and Spades	132
Up in the Clouds	62	Along the Route of the Great Central	134
We Never Closed	64	Land of Plenty	136
British Standard Gauge		Index	139
Passenger-Carrying Heritage			
Railways	66		

EXETER ST DAVID'S
by Frederick Thomas

St David's station – fifteen after seven.
A splendid structure; really, 'tis a pity
They didn't build it closer to the city,
For one can almost fancy on the spot
He's in the Midlands, where of course he's not.
But hark! the bell has gone, the whistle sounds,
The engine creaks, and from the station bounds.
And here a gleam of sunshine, warm and bright,
Bursts on St David's Vale, as comes in sight
The ancient city, with its many spires...

THE JOY OF TRAINSPOTTING
How one small boy fell in love with trains

As a young child I couldn't fail to get excited about railways. Born in Gloucester, for many years I lived just across the road from the old Midland Railway main line from Eastgate Station to Bristol. Behind our house and just across the park was the Docks branch, worked by the diminutive MR Deeley 0-4-0s, complete with driver's bicycle slung over the front buffers. Along this line also trundled brand new London Underground trains, narrow gauge carriages for far-flung railways of the British empire and, later, sparkling new single-car diesel multiple units for British Railways – all of these emerging from the Gloucester Railway Carriage & Wagon Works like full-size Airfix kits.

As a youngster I attended Tredworth Road Junior School and to get there entailed crossing the Midland main line either at Painswick Road or Farm Street Crossings. Inevitably, my perambulations were often interrupted by the passage of a train, sometimes a long slow goods train hauled by a '4F' or '8F' belching steam and smoke as it tackled the gradient out of Gloucester. At other times there was the sheer excitement of seeing a named train, usually hauled by a 'Jubilee' or a 'Black Five', such as the 'Pines Express' or the 'Devonian'.

'Behind our house was the Docks branch, worked by the diminutive MR Deeley 0-4-0s, complete with driver's bicycle slung over the front buffers.'

At home my father had built me (or was it really for himself?) a splendid '0' gauge layout on trestles around one of our attics. With Horny and Bassett-Lowke locos racing around the tracks and the sound of a 'Jubilee' passing outside on the Bristol to Newcastle mail train, how could a small boy not be totally absorbed in railways?

My father didn't have a car (nor a TV or phone) and because of this my holidays were pure bliss. Each year we usually had one week's holiday in either Swanage, Lyme Regis, Exmouth or Woolacombe and the journey there and back was the highlight of the whole week. My favourite journey was to Lyme Regis. Invariably, this entailed lugging our suitcases down to Eastgate Station where we would catch a stopping train for Mangotsfield, usually hauled by a '2P' 4-4-0. Here, at this draughty triangular station, we would alight to await the train for Bath Green Park. What a delightful station Bath GP was – wooden platforms and an overall roof (it's still there as a covered parking area for Sainsbury's!). The next stage of our epic journey was over the Mendips on the

'Back at home my father had built me (or was it really for himself?) a splendid "O" gauge layout on trestles around one of our attics.'

Slow and Dirty to Templecombe. Apart from smoky Devonshire tunnels, I would usually spend the rest of the trip with my head out of the window, much to my mother's concern. Templecombe was very exciting as I watched the 'Merchant Navies' thunder through at great speed on their switchback ride between Exeter and Waterloo.

During a lull between the holiday expresses we would embark on the fourth stage of our journey to Axminster where we would make our final change on to the Lyme Regis branch. Invariably the train was hauled by one of the veteran Adams radial tanks, which wound its way through leafy cuttings and across Cannington Viaduct before depositing us and our luggage at our destination.

If only I had a time machine. . .

I distinctly remember the first time I went trainspotting. Having just passed my 11-plus exam I went on to attend the Crypt Grammar School where several of my classmates had already been bitten by the craze. I was determined that one Saturday I would catch the bus to Gloucester Central station to investigate this phenomenon. I have still got my *Sterling No.*

Standard Class '5' 4-6-0 No. 73094 passing Tramway Junction, Gloucester, with a train of empty iron ore tipplers, 31 March 1965

3 notebook from that portentous day in 1957 when I hung around Central Station, taking in the smell of smoke, steam and oil – it was like being let loose in a sweetshop! Here are the first locomotives that I ever spotted:

2242, 2826, 7208, 7810 *Draycott Manor*, 7920 *Coney Hall*, 5042 *Winchester Castle*, 4085 *Berkeley Castle*, 6838 *Goodmoor Grange*, 4088 *Dartmouth Castle*, 5917 *Westminster Hall*, 5914 *Ripon Hall*, 2266, 4139, 2227, 5418, 6394, 6354, 5017 *The Gloucestershire Regiment 28th. 61st*, 3848, 2815, 73011, 1631, 6354, 5041 *Tiverton Castle*, 6865 *Hopton Grange*.

There used to be a long footbridge spanning a multitude of carriage and wagon sidings that connected Gloucester Central and Eastgate stations. I wandered over this on to the platform at Eastgate and here are the locomotives that I spotted there:

73073, 73054, 48523, 41078, 44045, 44818, 58165, 44757, 43932, 1605, 44962.

Needless to say, after that first trip I got the bug really badly and soon I was travelling far and wide to Swindon Works, Derby Works and Bristol. Gloucester was a fascinating place with the comings and goings of both WR and LMR expresses, coal trains from and iron ore trains to South Wales, local workings to Hereford and Bristol, the Chalford push-pull plus all of the local traffic from the docks, carriage and wagon works and gas works. It was not unusual to see a gleaming ex-works WR loco running in on a Swindon stopping train and one of the highlights of each day was the 'Cornishman' express, its brown and cream coaches hauled by an immaculate Wolverhampton Stafford Road (84A) 'Castle' Class loco such as No. 5050 *Earl of Dudley*.

One of my craziest and last trips took place on the early morning of 8 May 1966 when, after staying with friends in London, I caught the 00.15 train out of Euston behind one of the newly introduced AC electrics, E3122. The purpose of this journey was to travel back to London via the Great Central main line, which was due for imminent closure.

After alighting at Rugby Midland in the wee hours of the morning, I walked across to a completely deserted Rugby Central where I caught the York to Swindon train hauled by Hymek diesel-hydraulic D7093. In the company of a couple of railway workers, I travelled down to Woodford Halse where I alighted before the train set off again for its journey to Swindon via Banbury and Didcot. The Great Central was in its death throes. Woodford Halse in the middle of the night was a pretty scary place to be on your own! The once-busy station was

> *'After that first trip I got the bug really badly
> and soon I was travelling far and wide.'*

completely deserted, there were no lights and I was the only passenger waiting for the early morning train to Marylebone. It duly arrived and I am sure that the driver of D5016 looked astonished as he spotted me waiting on the gloomy platform. The last leg of the journey to Marylebone was duly completed and I returned to my friends' flat in St John's Wood – nobody was any the wiser about

'Jubilee' Class 4-6-0 No 45565 Victoria, Eastgate Station, 1964

A 'Castle' Class 4-6-0 ready to leave Gloucester Central in 1959

my night-time antics as they were all still asleep! The Great Central was itself finally put to sleep only four months later.

I cannot think of any subject as fascinating as the history of Britain's railways. Witness the thousands of books that have already been written, ranging from weighty tomes on subjects such as the Great Western Railway to slim volumes on more esoteric subjects such as the Lincolnshire Potato Railways. There is obviously an audience out there that can still remember our glorious railways before they were destroyed by politicians!

This little book is meant to be dipped into at random and read in any order. From 'Fair Exchange', 'How Rats Ruined a Railway' and 'The Dockers' Umbrella' to 'Warships and Westerns', 'From Gunboats to Corpses', and 'The Streakers', the choice of subjects is wide-ranging and there will hopefully be something that will fascinate even the most ardent enthusiast or historian.

Enjoy it!

CRASH!
The story of Britain's worst railway disaster

It was just gone six o'clock on the morning of 22 May 1915 and George Meakin was nearing the end of his night shift as signalman at Quintinshill, a small block post on the main line, 10 miles north of Carlisle. The two overnight expresses from Euston to Glasgow, running late, were due and a slow-running northbound goods train was already waiting patiently in the down loop line for them to pass before resuming its journey. However, a local passenger train had already left Carlisle ahead of the two expresses and, as the down loop was already occupied, Meakin switched the local train on to the up main line where it came to a halt close to his signalbox. Finally, to complete this busy scene, a Carlisle-bound goods train was directed into the up loop line just as Meakin's colleague, James Tinsley, arrived to start his shift.

On this morning, these two made a fatal error: forgetting the local train was standing on the up main line, they sent a signal to the next signalbox at Kirkpatrick which indicated that the up line was clear. Tinsley also pulled the signals to clear the passage of the northbound Euston to Glasgow express.

Tinsley, who arrived for work on the local train, always started his shift half an hour late and this was covered up by Meakin who, instead of recording train movements for this period in the official register, wrote these details for his mate on a separate piece of paper so they could be copied in later.

There next followed the most appalling sequence of events that culminated in Britain's worst ever rail disaster. With the signals cleared, a crowded troop train consisting of 15 old wooden coaches, all lit by acetylene gas, was now approaching Quintinshill on the up line at speed. It ran head-on into the stationary local with such an enormous force that the wooden coaches of the troop train were completely smashed to pieces and the locomotives ended up on their sides straddling the down main line. This in itself was a major disaster, but worse was to follow. One minute later, the first of the late-running down expresses, hauled by two locomotives and weighing over 600 tons, approached Quintinshill at high speed and ploughed into the debris of the first accident. Colliding with the tender of the troop train engine, the leading engine of the down express left the rails and came into collision with the stationary goods train waiting in the down loop line.

This total devastation was then turned into a scene from hell when the escaping gas from the smashed troop-train carriages was ignited by the red hot coals thrown out from the derailed locomotives.

In all, 227 people, of whom 215 were soldiers from the Royal Scots Regiment, lost their lives and a further 245 were injured, but because of wartime reporting restrictions, the accident was not widely publicised. At a later trial, both Meakin and Tinsley were found guilty of grossly neglecting their duties and also of culpable homicide, and were jailed for 18 months and three years respectively.

Diagram of the tracks and signals just prior to the accident

Table of Worst Railway Accidents

DATE	LOCATION	DEATHS/INJURIES	CAUSE
24 December 1841	Sonning	8/17	Landslip
20 August 1868	Abergele	33	Collision and fire
3 August 1873	Wigan	10	Derailment
10 September 1874	Norwich Thorpe	25/100	Collision
21 January 1876	Abbots Ripton	14	Collision in snow
28 December 1879	Tay Bridge	75	Bridge collapse
16 July 1884	Penistone	24	Derailment
12 June 1889	Armagh	80	Collision
10 November 1890	Norton Fitzwarren	10	Collision
1 September 1905	Witham	11	Derailment
1 July 1906	Salisbury	28	Derailment
2 September 1913	Ais Gill	14/38	Collision and fire
22 May 1915	Quintinshill	227/245	Collision and fire
27 June 1928	Darlington	25	Collision
13 October 1928	Charfield	15	Collision and fire
28 September 1934	Winwick Junction	12	Collision
10 December 1937	Castle Cary	35/179	Collision in snow
4 November 1940	Norton Fitzwarren	27	Derailment
30 September 1945	Bourne End	43/64	Derailment
24 October 1947	South Croydon	32/183	Collision
8 October 1952	Harrow & Wealdstone	112/340	Collision in fog
23 January 1955	Sutton Coldfield	17/43	Derailment
2 December 1955	Barnes	13/41	Collision and fire
4 December 1957	Lewisham	90/173	Collision
30 January 1958	Dagenham East	10/89	Collision
5 November 1967	Hither Green	49/78	Derailment
11 June 1972	Eltham Well Hall	6/126	Derailment
20 December 1973	Ealing	10/94	Derailment
28 February 1975	Moorgate	43	Collision with buffer stops
12 December 1988	Clapham Common	35/100	Collision
4 March 1989	Purley	6/94	Collision
8 January 1991	Cannon Street	2/200	Collision with buffer stops
19 September 1997	Southall	6/150	Collision
5 October 1999	Ladbroke Grove	31/523	Collision
17 October 2000	Hatfield	4/35	Derailment
28 February 2001	Selby	10/80	Collision with car
10 May 2002	Potters Bar	7/70	Derailment
6 November 2004	Ufton Nervet	7/150	Collision with car

A LOCAL TRAIN OF THOUGHT
By Siegfried Sassoon

Alone, in silence, at a certain time of night,
Listening, and looking up from what I'm trying to write,
I hear a local train along the Valley, And 'There
Goes the one-fifty,' think I to myself; aware
That somehow its habitual travelling comforts me,
Making my world seem safer, homelier, sure to be
The same tomorrow; and the same, one hopes, next year.
'There's peacetime in that train.' One hears it disappear
With needless warning whistle and rail-resounding wheels.
'That train's quite like an old familiar friend,' one feels.

AN ECCENTRIC RAILWAY EMPIRE
The Story of Colonel H.F. Stephens and his light railways

Holman Fred Stephens, the son of the Pre-Raphaelite artist Frederic George Stephens, was born in 1868 and went on to become a leading exponent of the building and managing of light railways in England and Wales. As a student he attended University College, London, where he studied civil engineering before enrolling as an apprentice engineer at the Metropolitan Railway's Neasden Works in 1881. Following his apprenticeship, Stephens went on to hold the post of assistant engineer during the construction of the Cranbrook & Paddock Wood Railway, which opened on 1 October 1892.

As an associate member of the Institute of Civil Engineers from 1894, Stephens was allowed to design and construct railways and he wasted no time setting about his first project. In anticipation of the passing of the 1896 Light Railways Act, which allowed the building of low-cost and lightly constructed railways in lightly populated, rural areas, Stephens formed a company, known as the Light Railway Syndicate, with his friend Edward Peterson in 1895. Designed to obtain orders for new light railways, the company claimed to have potential investors. In reality this was not so and, although seven light railway schemes were proposed by the company, only one, the Sheppey Light Railway, which opened in 1901 between Queenborough and Leysdown-on-Sea, was actually built.

Despite his failure to obtain contracts for the Light Railway

Sheerness Line

- Leysdown
- Harty Road
- Eastchurch
- Brambledown Halt
- Minster On Sea
- East Minster On Sea
- Sheerness East
- Sheerness Line *to Sheerness-on-Sea*
- Queenborough
- Sheerness Line *to Sittingbourne and Chatham Main Line*

Syndicate, Stephens was highly successful building and managing railways in his own right. His first, the 2-mile, narrow gauge Rye & Camber Tramway, was opened in 1895 and preceded the Light Railways Act by one year. His first light railway, the Rother Valley between Robertsbridge and Rolvenden in Kent, was opened on 2 April 1900 and was the first railway to be built under the provisions of the 1896 Light Railway Act. In addition to building and managing many lines in England and Wales (see table overleaf), Stephens twice extended his Rother Valley Railway, now known as the Kent & East Sussex Railway, first to Tenterden in 1903 and finally to Headcorn in 1905.

Between 1900 and his sudden death in 1931, Stephens ran his railway empire from a modest office at 23 Salford Terrace in nearby Tonbridge. On his death, his second-in-command, William Henry Austen took over the far-flung railway empire, but the writing was soon on the wall for these, by now, ramshackle rural railways. Increased competition from buses brought about the termination of many passenger services, leaving just a skeleton goods service operated by second-hand and antique locos.

By 1948 most of these idyllic little lines had closed and only three – the Kent & East Sussex (now a successful preserved railway), the East Kent and the Shropshire & Montgomeryshire – became part of the nationalised and newly formed British Railways.

Alongside his railway business interests, which would have taken up most men's energy alone, Stephens also found time for a military career. He first came into contact with the Army when he joined the University College School cadet company in 1888 and received his first commission in 1896 when he became second lieutenant with the 1st Sussex (Volunteer) Royal Engineers. He rose through the ranks and by 1916, when he received a Mention in Despatches, had been promoted to Lieutenant-Colonel Royal Engineers (Territorial Reserve). Stephens finally retired from Army life in 1925.

The 'Colonel Stephens' Railways

Paddock Wood & Cranbrook Railway
Route: Paddock Wood – Hawkhurst
Distance: 11½ miles

After completing his apprenticeship with the Metropolitan Railway, Stephens was appointed resident engineer during the line's construction between 1890 and 1894. The railway was taken over by the South Eastern & Chatham Railway in 1900 and closed in 1961.

The Hundred of Manhood & Selsey Tramway
Route: Chichester – Selsey
Distance: 8 miles

Built and managed by Stephens, this agricultural light railway was opened to Selsey Town in 1897. It was further extended to Selsey Beach in 1908 but, due to road competition, the line was closed in 1935.

Kent & East Sussex Railway
Route: Robertsbridge – Headcorn
Distance: 21 miles

Built, owned and managed by Stephens, this line was opened between Robertsbridge and Rolvenden in 1900, Rolvenden to Tenterden in 1902 and finally to Headcorn in 1905. Although serving a sparsely populated rural area the railway struggled on into nationalisation in 1948. All passenger traffic ceased in 1953 and the section between Tenterden to Headcorn

was closed. The remainder of the railway closed in 1961. The section between Tenterden Town and Bodiam has now been reopened as a preserved line.

The Sheppey Light Railway
Route: Queenborough – Leysdown-on-Sea
Distance: 8½ miles

Engineered by Stephens, this railway was opened in 1901 and owned and operated by the South Eastern & Chatham Railway from 1905. Struggling through to become part of British Railways in 1948, the railway finally closed in 1950.

Bere Alston & Calstock Railway and East Cornwall Mineral Railway
Route: Bere Alston – Callington

Working with Messrs Galbraith & Church, Stephens designed and equipped this railway, including converting a former narrow gauge mineral line and constructing the graceful viaduct across the Tamar at Calstock. Opened in 1908, the section from Gunnislake to Callington was closed in 1966 but the remainder is still open to passengers as a branch line from Plymouth.

Burry Port & Gwendraeth Valley Railway
Route: Burry Port – Cwm Mawr
Distance: 12 miles

Between 1909 and 1913 Stephens was

responsible for upgrading this hitherto mineral line to passenger-carrying standards. The railway became part of the GWR in 1923 and passenger traffic ceased in 1953. Remnants of the line were kept in use for coal traffic until 1996.

Shropshire & Montgomeryshire Light Railway
Route: Shrewsbury Abbey – Llanymynech and a branch from Kinnerley Junction to Criggion
Distance: 24 miles

Opened originally in 1866 as the Potteries, Shrewsbury & North Wales Railway, this line was closed in 1880 due to financial difficulties. Seeing an opportunity, Stephens took over the dormant railway in 1907 and rebuilt it to light railway standards. Also owned and managed by Stephens, the line, renamed the Shropshire & Montgomeryshire Light Railway, opened for business in 1911. Passenger services ceased in 1933 and the railway lingered on until it was taken over by the military in 1941. Nationalised in 1948, the line remained on lease to the military until closure in 1960.

Weston, Clevedon & Portishead Railway
Route: Weston-super-Mare (Ashcombe Road) to Portishead
Distance: 14 miles

Originally built as a tramway, the line was converted to a light railway in 1907. From 1911 until its closure in 1940, the line was managed by Stephens and his successor, W.H. Austen.

East Kent Light Railway
Route: Shepherdswell – Wingham and a branch from Eastry to Richborough Port.
Distance: 18 miles

Designed, built and managed by Stephens, this line opened for coal traffic from the Kent coalfield in 1911. Passenger services commenced in 1916 and ceased in 1948 when the railway became part of British Railways. By 1951 most of the line had been completely closed with only the section to Tilmanstone Colliery remaining open until 1986. Today, a short section from Shepherdswell to Eythorne is run as a preserved line.

Edge Hill Light Railway
Route: Burton Dassett Junction – Edge Hill Quarry
Distance: 3½ miles

Designed to carry ironstone, the short-lived, freight-only Edge Hill Light Railway was engineered by Stephens in 1919. Opened in 1922 and incorporating a cable-worked incline, the railway was never a success due to the poor quality of the ironstone. The line closed in 1925.

Snailbeach District Railway
Route: Pontesbury – Snailbeach
Distance: 3 miles

Originally opened in 1877, this narrow gauge line was built to convey lead ore from mines in the Stipperstones Hills in Shropshire. Although initially a successful commercial enterprise, traffic had declined to such a low point that by the 1920s it had almost ceased to operate. Then, in 1923, Stephens purchased the line and set about re-equipping it and bringing it back to life. The opening of a stone quarry and a stone-crushing plant to supply the county council with road building material brought increased traffic and through the 1930s the line prospered. In 1947 the line was leased to Shropshire County Council who continued to operate part of it until final closure in 1959.

Ffestiniog Railway
Route: Porthmadog – Blaenau Ffestiniog
Distance: 13½ miles

This pioneering Welsh narrow gauge railway, originally opened to convey slate in 1836, had by the end of World War I fallen on hard times. To revive the railway's fortunes, Stephens was appointed manager in 1923 and chairman in 1925 until his death in 1931. At the same time he automatically became manager of the Welsh Highland Railway which was then under the same ownership as the Ffestiniog. His successor, W. H. Austen, continued in this role until he resigned in 1936. Their timely intervention almost certainly saved the Ffestiniog Railway from early closure. The railway ceased to operate in 1946 but was brought back to life by a group of dedicated enthusiasts and is now one of the premier tourist attractions in North Wales – for the full story see pages 130–1. The Welsh Highland Railway closed in 1936 but has since reopened as a tourist line between Caernarfon and Porthmadog (see page 78).

Ashover Light Railway
Route: Clay Cross – Ashover
Distance: 7 miles

Engineered by Stephens, this narrow gauge line was opened in 1924 to convey stone for the Clay Cross Company. Passenger services ceased in 1936 and the line closed completely in 1950.

North Devon & Cornwall Junction Light Railway
Route: Great Torrington – Halwill Junction
Distance: 20 miles

Rebuilt partly from an existing narrow gauge china clay line, this railway was engineered and managed by Stephens until its opening in 1925 when it came under the operational control of the Southern Railway. Becoming part of British Railways in 1948, the line closed to passengers throughout and to goods between Halwill and Meeth in 1965. The northern section from Great Torrington to Meeth stayed open for china clay traffic until 1982.

TO A GREAT WESTERN BROAD GAUGE ENGINE AND ITS STOKER
By Horatio Brown

So! I shall never see you more,
You mighty lord of railway-roar;
The splendid stroke of driving-wheel,
The burnished brass, the shining steel,
Triumphant pride of him who drives
From Paddington to far St Ives,
Another year, and then your place
Knows you no more; a pygmy race
Usurps the glory of the road,
And trails along a lesser load.
Drive on the engine, drive amain,
Wrap me, like love, yet once again
A follower in your fiery train.

Drive on! and driving, let me know
The golden West, its warmth, its glow.
Pass Thames with all his winding maze;
Sweet Clifton dreaming in a haze;

And, farther yet, pass Taunton Vale,
And Dawlish rocks, and Teignmouth sail,
And Totnes, where the dancing Dart
Comes seaward with a gladsome heart;
Then let me feel the wind blow free
From levels of the Cornish sea.

Drive on! let all your fiery soul,
Your puissant heart that scorns control,
Your burnished limbs of circling steel,
The throb, the pulse of driving-wheel,
O'erflood the breast of him whose gaze
Is set to watch your perilous ways,
Burn brighter in those eyes of vair,
Blow back the curly, close-cropped hair,
Ah! Western lad, would I might be
A partner in that ecstasy.

A BRIDGE TOO FAR
The story of the Tay Bridge disaster

It was the night of Sunday, 28 December 1879 and a Force 10 gale was blowing up the Firth of Tay. Having previously crossed the Firth of Forth by ferry on their journey from Edinburgh, the 75 passengers travelling on to Dundee joined their train at Burntisland and set off into the dark night. Pausing at St Fort for their tickets to be collected, the passengers settled down for the last leg of their journey across the newly opened Tay Bridge. From the St Fort signal box, the signalman watched as the train's red tail light receded into the windswept darkness as it passed on to the bridge.

Designed by Thomas Bouch, Tay Bridge was constructed out of 85 cast-iron lattice-grid spans supported on cast-iron columns and strengthened with wrought-iron struts and ties. To allow shipping to pass under the bridge, 13 spans, known as the High Girders, were built higher than the rest of the bridge and were approached on each side up a gradient that varied between 1 in 74 and 1 in 130. During tests in 1878, a number of locomotives were coupled together and safely ran over the bridge at speeds of 40mph. However, the effect of high winds on a train passing over such an exposed structure was unknown.

The 75 doomed passengers, including Thomas Bouch's son-in-law travelling on the Burntisland to Dundee train, never reached their destination. As it started to cross the High Girders, the force of the gale-force winds sweeping up the Tay estuary brought about the collapse of the centre section of the spans, and the train and its passengers plunged into the icy waters of the Tay.

Built to shorten the railway journey between Edinburgh and Aberdeen, the Tay Bridge was officially opened by Queen Victoria on 1 June 1878. Taking nearly seven years to build, the 2¼-mile single-track bridge was an enormous feat of engineering and, when completed, was the longest railway bridge in the world.

Fallen Tay Bridge from the north

A view of the original Tay Bridge from Dundee

Confusion reigned at Dundee station when the train didn't arrive, and two railway workers volunteered to crawl along the bridge to ascertain the problem. Crawling on all fours in a howling gale, they found that a section of the bridge had disappeared, and returned with the news everyone was dreading.

At the official inquiry into the disaster, it was concluded that the bridge collapsed due to a combination of bad design, construction and maintainance, and that there were inherent weaknesses in the wrought-iron tie bars that secured the spans to the supporting columns – in short, it was an accident waiting to happen. The blame fell squarely on the bridge's designer and engineer, Sir Thomas Bouch, and he died a broken man less than a year afterwards. A new double-track railway bridge was eventually opened in 1887 alongside the line of the original bridge, and it remains in use today.

> The only survivor of the disaster was the North British Railway's 4-4-0 No. 224, which was lifted from the river bed, repaired and returned to service.

HOW RATS RUINED A RAILWAY
The story of Brunel's atmospheric South Devon Railway

Isambard Kingdom Brunel, not a man to ignore the latest technology, had just completed the building of the Bristol & Exeter Railway. His next project was to extend the railway line from Exeter to Plymouth, which would involve some steep gradients west of Newton Abbot. Concerned about the steam locomotive's ability to pull heavy trains on this section, in 1844 he made the decision to build an atmospheric railway.

> The atmospheric system had been patented by Clegg, Samuda and Samuda in 1838, and on witnessing early trials in West London, Brunel was highly impressed with the results.

Obviating the need for normal steam locomotives, the system consisted of a 20in-diameter iron pipe located between the rails from which stationary steam engines pumped out air to create a vacuum. The iron pipe had a slot in the top, sealed by a leather flap, and a 15ft-long piston, secured on a rod beneath the leading carriage, fitted into the pipe. The pressure of the air that was sucked into the vacuum pipe as the flap was opened moved the piston, and the train, forwards. As the piston moved forwards, two small wheels in front of and behind it first opened the flap and then resealed it. Stationary pumping houses located at intervals of 3 miles along the line were used to ensure a permanent vacuum was kept in the pipe.

Unfortunately, the equipment for the atmospheric railway had not been delivered when the railway opened as far as Teignmouth on 30 May 1846 and locomotives, hired from the Great Western Railway, had to be used to haul trains. The next section of line to Newton Abbot was opened on 30 December

1846 but there was still no sign of the atmospheric equipment. Finally, in February 1847, enough equipment had been delivered for Brunel to start trials with the system. Although fairly successful with lightly loaded trains, problems were encountered at this early stage with early deterioration of the leather flap that was supposed to keep the pipe air-tight. Tallow (grease that was produced from melting animal fat) was liberally applied to the slot in the pipe in an effort to ensure an air-tight seal, but it was soon found that it melted in hot sunshine and that rats found it tasty!

Route of the atmospheric system

Finally, passenger-carrying atmospheric trains started operation between Exeter and Teignmouth on 13 September 1847 and were extended to Newton Abbot on 10 January 1848. On 23 February, all trains, including freight, were operating on the atmospheric system. By July the system was operating as far as Totnes and work went ahead to complete the remaining steeply graded section to Plymouth. However, escalating costs due to the high maintenance required to ensure an air-tight seal, along with the system's eccentric uniqueness, soon brought about its demise. A more or less unanimous vote to abandon the system was taken by South Devon Railway shareholders at the end of August and it ceased to operate on 6 September 1848.

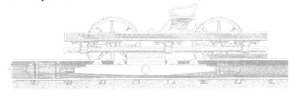

The atmospheric system

BIRTH AND DEATH OF A RAILWAY
The story of the Lyme Regis branch

The Dorset seaside town of Lyme Regis, with its ancient Cobb Harbour, had been an important trading centre since medieval times. By the mid-18th century it had also become a popular destination for artists, poets, writers and royalty. Mary Anning's discovery of important dinosaur fossils in the crumbling clay cliffs on either side of the town in 1799 brought it more fame, and by the early 19th century it had become a popular resort for the wealthy.

Despite its growth and although the London & South Western Railway's line from Yeovil to Exeter had opened in July 1860, Lyme Regis had to wait another 43 years before it was connected to the main line at Axminster.

Although there were several schemes to build a railway to Lyme Regis, nothing was done until the passing of the Light Railways Act in 1896. This Act enabled the building of low-cost and lightly constructed railways in sparsely populated rural areas, and soon many optimistic schemes were being put forward to build such lines throughout the country. One of these was the Axminster & Lyme Regis Light Railway Company, which obtained a Light Railway Order in 1899. The company appointed Arthur Pain as its engineer and work

Adams radial 4-4-2 tank loco at Combpyne station

started on the construction of the line in 1900. Although the steeply graded 6¾-mile line was built to light railway standards, there was still one major engineering feat that needed to be accomplished: the ten-arch viaduct across the valley at Cannington. One of the earliest viaducts in the country to be built of concrete, material for the structure arrived by sea at Cobb Harbour in Lyme Regis. However, during construction, one of the arches suffered an unforeseen settlement and had to be reinforced by an unsightly jack arch. Once these problems had been overcome, the railway was opened on 24 August 1903 with the first train being double-headed by 'Terrier' Class 0-6-0s Nos 734 and 735. Apart from the terminus at Lyme Regis, located high above the town, and the junction with the main line at Axminster, there was only one intermediate station, Combpyne.

From the outset, train services were operated by the London & South Western Railway which, in 1907, took over the line completely. The company then proceeded to upgrade the branch by installing signalling and relaying the track with conventional rail. Passenger traffic on the branch was heavy during the summer months but by the time of the Big Four Railway Grouping in 1923, when the L&SWR became part of the larger Southern Railway, competition from road transport was already being felt. The location of the terminus at Lyme Regis, 250ft above sea level, necessitating a long walk uphill from the town, certainly did not help the situation. Goods traffic, including livestock, fertilisers and large quantities of coal, was frequently attached to the regular passenger train to form a mixed train.

Under the Southern Railway, the Lyme Regis branch saw the weekday summer service increase to 11 trains each way per day, and from 1930, a Sunday service also operated. The winter Sunday service continued until the autumn of 1951 when it was replaced by a bus service that connected with main line trains at Axminster station. The growth of summer holiday traffic after World War II also saw the introduction of through coaches between London Waterloo and Lyme Regis. This service ran from 1953 until 1963 with coaches often being conveyed in one of the many portions of the 'Atlantic Coast Express' before being detached or attached at Axminster. In its final summer of operation this train left Waterloo at 10.45am and, after pausing at tiny Combpyne station, arrived at Lyme Regis at 2.13pm – the equivalent car journey today along our congested roads would probably take longer. So much for progress!

Locomotive haulage on this steeply graded and sharply curved line was initially in the hands of the diminutive ex-London Brighton & South Coast Railway's A1 'Terrier' Class 0-6-0s, but these were replaced by the ancient ex-L&SWR Adams radial 4-4-2 tank engines as early as 1913. Three of these endearing locomotives, all built in 1885, continued to provide the mainstay of motive power on the line until 1961 when they were replaced by more modern ex-LMS Class '2MT' 2-6-2 tanks. These steam locomotives were based at Exmouth Junction shed at Exeter where they returned once a week for routine maintenance. Steam haulage ended in November 1963 and goods services were withdrawn soon after. From then until closure, a much reduced passenger service was handled by two-car and, finally, single-car diesel multiple units. Despite much local opposition, the line closed completely on 29 November 1965.

Attempts to reopen part of the line in 1970 came to nothing and now Lyme Regis suffers from traffic gridlock in its narrow streets and appalling car-parking problems during summer weekends. Bring back the railway!

THE RAILWAY JUNCTION
By Walter de la Mare

From here through tunnelled gloom the track
Forks into two; and one of these
Wheels onward into darkening hills,
And one towards distant seas.

How still it is; the signal light
At set of sun shines palely green;
A thrush sings; other sound there's none,
Nor traveller to be seen—

Where late there was a throng. And now,
In peace awhile, I sit alone;
Though soon, at the appointed hour,
I shall myself be gone.

But not their way: the bow-legged groom,
The parson in black, the widow and son,
The sailor with his cage, the gaunt
Gamekeeper with his gun,

That fair one, too, discreetly veiled
All, who so mutely came, and went,
Will reach those far nocturnal hills,
Or shores, ere night is spent.

I nothing know why thus we met—
Their thoughts, their longings, hopes, their fate:
And what shall I remember, except—
The evening growing late—

That here through tunnelled gloom the track
Forks into two; of these
One into darkening hills leads on,
And one towards distant seas?

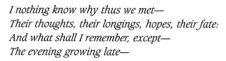

FIND YOUR LOCAL SHED CODE!

Individual locomotives have always been assigned to a specific engine shed. This was their home, where they always returned after their spell of duty. Here they were cleaned and maintained and quite often became a source of local pride. Some locomotives that were named after local heroes often spent their whole lives based at the same shed. For instance, 'Castle' Class 4-6-0 No. 5017 *The Gloucestershire Regiment 28th, 61st*, was named after the local regiment when it returned from battle in the Korean War, and was based at Gloucester (Horton Road) shed until the end of its days.

Each engine shed was given a code, for instance Gloucester (Horton Road) was 85B, and locomotives assigned to that shed carried the code on a cast-iron plate fixed to the bottom of the smokebox door. Smaller sheds, or sub-sheds, were not given separate codes as the locomotives that used these came under the control of the local mother shed; Brimscombe was a sub-shed of Gloucester (Horton Road), for example. Following are the shed codes that were used by British Railways in the summer of 1961. Can you find your local shed code?

A Standard '9F' 2-10-0 takes on water at Gloucester (Horton Road)

The London & South Western Railway engine shed, Bournemouth, 1928

British Railways' Shed Codes (Summer 1961)

LONDON MIDLAND REGION

1A Willesden
1B Camden
1C Watford
1D Devons Road (Bow)
1E Bletchley
    Leighton Buzzard

2A Rugby
2B Nuneaton
2E Northampton
2F Woodford Halse

5A North
5B Crewe South
5C Stafford
5D Stoke
5E Alsager
5F Uttoxeter

6A Chester (Midland)
6B Mold Junction
6C Birkenhead
6F Bidston
6G Llandudno Junction
6H Bangor
6J Holyhead
6K Rhyl

8A Edge Hill (Liverpool)
8B Warrington (Dallam)
8C Speke Junction
8D Widnes
8E Northwich
8F Springs Bank
    (Wigan)
8G Sutton Oak

9A Longsight
    (Manchester)
9B Stockport (Edgeley)
9C Macclesfield

9D Buxton
9E Trafford Park
    Glazebrook
9F Heaton Mersey
    Gowhole
9G Gorton
    Dinting
    Reddish

12A Carlisle (Kingmoor)
12B Carlisle (Upperby)
    Penrith
12C Carlisle (Canal)
12D Kirkby Stephen
12E Barrow
12F Workington
12G Oxenholme
12H Tebay

14A Cricklewood
14B Kentish Town
14D Neasden
    Aylesbury
14E Bedford

15A Wellingborough
15B Kettering
15C Leicester (Midland)
15D Coalville
15E Leicester (Central)
15F Market Harborough

16A Nottingham
16B Kirkby-in-Ashfield
16D Annesley

17A Derby
17B Burton
    Overseal
17C Rowsley
    Cromford
    Middleton
    Sheep Pasture

18A Toton (Stapleford
    & Sandiacre)
18B Westhouses
18C Hasland

21A Saltley
21B Bescot
21C Bushbury
21D Aston
21E Monument Lane
21F Walsall

24A Accrington
24B Rose Grove
24C Lostock Hall
24D Lower Darwen
24E Blackpool
24F Fleetwood
24G Skipton
24H Hellifield
24J Lancaster
    (Green Ayre)
24K Preston
24L Carnforth

26A Newton Heath
26B Agecroft
26C Bolton
26D Bury
26E Lees (Oldham)
26F Patricroft

27A Bank Hall
27B Aintree
27C Southport
27D Wigan
27E Walton-on-the-Hill
27F Brunswick
    (Liverpool)
    Warrington (Central)

EASTERN REGION

30A Stratford
    Bishops Stortford
    Chelmsford
    Enfield Town
    Hertford East
    Southend (Victoria)
    Wood Street
    (Walthamstow)
30E Colchester
    Clacton
    Maldon
    Walton-on-Naze
30F Parkeston

31A Cambridge
    Ely
31B Whitemoor
31C King's Lynn

32A Norwich (Thorpe)
    Cromer Beach
32B Ipswich
32C Lowestoft Central
32D Yarmouth South
    Town

33B Tilbury
33C Shoeburyness

34A King's Cross
34B Hornsey
34D Hitchin
34E New England
34F Grantham
34G Finsbury Park
36A Doncaster
36C Frodingham
36E Retford

40A Lincoln
40B Immingham
    Grimsby

New Holland
40E Colwick
40F Boston
    Sleaford

41A Sheffield (Darnall)
41B Sheffield
    (Grimesthorpe)
41C Millhouses
41D Canklow
41E Staveley
    (Barrow Hill)
41F Mexborough
41H Staveley (ex-G C)
41J Langwith

NORTH EASTERN REGION

50A York
50B Hull (Dairycoates)
    Hull (Alexandra
    Dock)
50C Hull (Botanic
    Gardens)
50D Goole
50E Scarborough
50F Malton

51A Darlington
51C West Hartlepool
51F West Auckland
51J Northallerton
51L Thornaby
52A Gateshead
    Bowes Bridge
52B Heaton
52C Blaydon
    Alston
52D Tweedmouth
    Alnmouth
52E Percy Main
52F North and South
    Blyth
52G Sunderland
52H Tyne Dock
    Pelton Level

52K Consett
55A Leeds (Holbeck)
55B Stourton
55C Farnley
55D Royston
55E Normanton
55F Bradford
    (Manningham)
    Keighley
55G Huddersfield
55H Leeds (Neville Hill)

56A Wakefield
    Knottingley
56B Ardsley
56C Copley Hill
56D Mirfield
56E Sowerby Bridge
56F Low Moor
56G Bradford
    (Hammerton St)

SCOTTISH REGION

60A Inverness
    Dingwall
    Kyle of Lochalsh
60B Aviemore
    Boat of Garten
60C Helmsdale
    Tain
60D Wick
    Thurso
61A Kittybrewster
    (Aberdeen)
    Ballater
    Fraserburgh
    Inverurie
    Peterhead
61B Aberdeen (Ferryhill)
61C Keith
    Banff
    Elgin

62A Thornton
    Anstruther
    Burntisland

Kirkcaldy
    Ladybank
    Methil
62B Dundee
    (Tay Bridge)
    Arbroath
    Montrose
    St Andrews
62C Dunfermline
    Alloa
    Kelty

63A Perth
    Aberfeldy
    Blair Atholl
    Crieff
    Forfar
63B Fort William
    Mallaig
63C Oban
    Ballachulish
64A St Margarets
    (Edinburgh)
    Dunbar
    Galashiels
    Hardengreen
    Longniddry
    North Berwick
    Seafield
    South Leith
64B Haymarket
64C Dalry Road
64F Bathgate
64G Hawick
64H Leith Central

65A Eastfield (Glasgow)
    Arrochar
65B St Rollox
65C Parkhead
65D Dawsholm
    Dumbarton
65E Kipps
65F Grangemouth
65G Yoker
65H Helensburgh
65I Balloch

65J Stirling
    Killin
65K Polmont

66A Polmadie
    (Glasgow)
66B Motherwell
66C Hamilton
66D Greenock
    (Ladyburn)
66E Carstairs

67A Corkerhill
    (Glasgow)
67B Hurlford
    Beith
    Muirkirk
67C Ayr
67D Ardrossan

68B Dumfries
68C Stranraer
68D Beattock

SOUTHERN REGION

70A Nine Elms
70B Feltham
70C Guildford
    Reading South
70D Basingstoke
70H Ryde (I O W)

71A Eastleigh
    Andover Junction
    Lymington
    Southampton
    Terminus
    Winchester
71B Bournemouth
    Branksome
71G Weymouth
    Bridport
71J Southampton
    Docks

72A Exmouth Junction
    Bude
    Callington
    Exmouth
    Lyme Regis
    Okehampton
    Seaton
72B Salisbury
72C Yeovil
72E Barnstaple
    Junction
    Ilfracombe
    Torrington
72F Wadebridge

73A Stewarts Lane
73B Bricklayers Arms
73C Hither Green
73E Faversham
73F Ashford (Kent)
    Gillingham (Kent)
    Ramsgate
73H Dover
    Folkestone
73J Tonbridge
75A Brighton
75B Redhill
75C Norwood Junction
75E Three Bridges
    Horsham
75F Tunbridge Wells
    West

WESTERN REGION

CED Cardiff East Dock

DG Danygraig Diesel
    Depot

81A Old Oak Common
81B Slough
81C Southall
81D Reading
81E Didcot
81F Oxford

    Fairford
82A Bristol (Bath Road)
82B St Philip's Marsh
    Bath
    Wells
    Weston-super-
      Mare
82C Swindon
    Chippenham
82D Westbury
    Frome
82E Bristol (Barrow
      Road)
82F Bath (Green Park)
    Radstock West
82F Templecombe

83A Newton Abbot
    Kingsbridge
83B Taunton
83C Exeter
    Tiverton Junction
83D Laira (Plymouth)
    Launceston
83E St Blazey
    Bodmin
    Moorswater
83F Truro
83G Penzance
    Helston
    St Ives
83H Plymouth (Friary)

84A Wolverhampton
    (Stafford Road)
84B Oxley
84C Banbury
84D Leamington Spa
84E Tyseley
    Stratford-on-Avon
84F Stourbridge
84G Kidderminster
84H Wellington (Salop)

85A Worcester
    Evesham
    Honeybourne

    Kingham
    Ledbury
85B Gloucester
    (Horton Road)
    Brimscombe
    Cheltenham
    (Malvern Road)
    Lydney
    Ross-on-Wye
85C Gloucester
    (Barnwood)
    Dursley
    Tewkesbury
85D Bromsgrove
    Redditch

86A Newport
    (Ebbw Junction)
86B Newport (Pill)
86C Hereford
86E Severn Tunnel
    Junction
86F Aberbeeg
86G Pontypool Road

87A Neath
    Glyn Neath
    Neath (N & B)
87B Duffryn Yard
87D Swansea East
    Dock
    Gurnos
    Upper Bank
87E Landore
87F Llanelly
    Burry Port
    Llandovery
    Pantyffnnon
87G Carmarthen
    Aberayron
87H Neyland
    Cardigan
    Milford Haven
    Pembroke Dock
    Whitland
87J Goodwick

88A Cardiff (Canton)
88B Cardiff (Radyr)
88C Barry
88D Merthyr
    Dowlais Cae Harris
    Rhymney
88E Abercynon
88F Treherbert
    Ferndale
88G Llantrisant
88H Tondu
88J Aberdare
88K Brecon

89A Shrewsbury
    Builth Road
    Craven Arms
    Knighton
    Leominster
89B Croes Newydd
89C Machynlleth
    Aberystwyth
    Aberystwyth
    (V of R)
    Porthmadog
    Pwllheli
89D Oswestry
    Llanidloes
    Moat Lane

BATTLE OF THE GAUGES
The rise and fall of Brunel's broad gauge

Why did Isambard Kingdom Brunel, chief engineer of the proposed Great Western Railway, opt for a gauge of 7ft 0¼in for his new line when all of the other railways being built in Britain at that time had a gauge of 4ft 8½in?

The latter gauge (minus half an inch) was originally adopted by George Stephenson when he built his first steam locomotive, the *Blucher*, for the Killingworth Colliery Railway in 1814. It then became the standard gauge in Britain and many other parts of the world and was also specified as a clause in Acts of Parliament that authorised the building of new railways.

However, this clause was somehow not included in the Great Western Railway Act of 1835, so Brunel, a man with innovative ideas, persuaded the GWR board of directors that a wider gauge would provide a much smoother and safer ride at higher speeds for its passengers than would the narrower gauge. The downside was that a wider gauge would not only add to the construction costs of the new line by taking up more land but would also increase friction on curves. Brunel's arguments obviously won the day and work started on his new broad gauge line from London Paddington to Bristol Temple Meads in 1837.

Based on the centuries-old measurement of the 5ft distance between the wheels of horse-drawn vehicles and then allowing for the width of the two rails, George Stephenson decided upon a gauge of 4ft 8in in 1814. The extra half inch was later added to reduce friction between wheel and rail.

The 116-mile long GWR line to Bristol was finally opened throughout on 30 June 1841, by which time construction costs had risen, mainly due to Brunel's exacting standards, from an estimated £3 million to £6 million. Over the ensuing years the GWR extended its broad gauge network to cover most of South West England and South Wales and also added mixed gauge lines to serve Birmingham. However, the rest of Britain's rapidly expanding railway network was operating to the narrower standard gauge and where these two gauges met at important trans-shipment junctions, such as Gloucester, chaos usually ensued. By 1861 there was even a mixed gauge line running into Paddington. Meanwhile, Brunel had died in 1859 and it was left to the able Daniel Gooch, formerly the GWR's locomotive engineer, to oversee the conversion from broad to standard gauge.

> By 1863 the GWR's total mileage was 1,105 miles so conversion was a major operation. This started in 1866 and by 1873 hundreds of miles of line in Oxfordshire, Berkshire, Wiltshire, Somerset, Hampshire and Wales had been relaid.

By the time Daniel Gooch died in 1889, only the main route from Paddington to Penzance via Bristol, plus a few Cornish branches, were still operating a broad gauge service. The conversion of this final section was a huge task –177 route miles of broad gauge and 252 route miles of mixed gauge – and was meticulously planned to take place over the weekend of 20–23 May 1892. Some 4,200 workmen with their tools and equipment were put into place along the route and all broad gauge locomotives and rolling stock made their last journey to an enormous scrap line at Swindon.

On the final day of operation, 20 May, the last broad gauge train to leave Paddington was the 5.00pm to Plymouth. Once it had passed, the permanent way engineers took over the line and the conversion operation to standard gauge was underway. All weekend they toiled and by 4.00am on Monday 23 May their work was complete. Brunel's broad gauge dream was over, but now the GWR could play an integral part as a major player in Britain's strategically important railway network.

FAMOUS LOCOMOTIVE ENGINEERS
Sir Nigel Gresley (1876–1941)

Class 'A4' 4-6-2 No. 60024 Kingfisher, *1966*

Herbert Nigel Gresley was born in Edinburgh on 19 June 1876 and brought up in the village of Netherseal in Derbyshire. While he was at Marlborough College he developed a love of railway engineering that was, in later life, to earn him his reputation as one of Britain's finest locomotive engineers.

After leaving Marlborough, the young Gresley was apprenticed at the London & North Western Railway's works at Crewe. To further his training he moved to the Lancashire & Yorkshire railway's works at Horwich, where he was taught by the famous engineer John Aspinall. After three years as Assistant Superintendent in the Carriage and Wagon Department at Newton Heath, Gresley was appointed Superintendent of the Carriage and Wagon Department of the Great Northern Railway in 1905. Six years later, at the age of 35, he succeeded H.A. Ivatt as the Locomotive Engineer of the Great Northern Railway.

In 1923 the Great Northern Railway became part of the new London & North Eastern Railway and Gresley was appointed Chief Mechanical Engineer, a position he held at LNER's Doncaster railway works until his death in 1941.

During his time at both the GNR and LNER, Gresley was responsible for 26 different locomotive designs including the 'A1' 4-6-2 in 1922, the 'A3' 4-6-2 in 1927 and the 'V2' 2-6-2 in 1936. His most famous locomotive must be the beautifully streamlined 'A4' 4-6-2 ,which first appeared in 1935. A locomotive of this class, No. 4468 *Mallard*, still holds the world speed record for steam locomotives, achieved in 1938 with a top speed of 126mph.

FROM A RAILWAY CARRIAGE
By Robert Louis Stevenson

Faster than fairies, faster than witches,
Bridges and houses, hedges and ditches;
And charging along like troops in a battle,
All through the meadows the horses and cattle:
All of the sights of the hill and the plain
Fly as thick as driving rain;
And ever again, in the wink of an eye,
Painted stations whistle by.

Here is a child who clambers and scrambles,
All by himself and gathering brambles;
Here is a tramp who stands and gazes;
And there is the green for stringing the daisies!
Here is a cart run away in the road
Lumping along with man and load;
And here is a mill and there is a river:
Each a glimpse and gone for ever!

FAMOUS LOCOMOTIVE ENGINEERS
Sir William Stanier (1876-1965)

William Arthur Stanier was born in Swindon on 27 May 1876. His father was the Chief Clerk to William Dean, then Locomotive Superintendent of the Great Western Railway, and, after completing his education in 1892, the young William Stanier also joined the GWR where he started work as an apprentice draughtsman. He was promoted to Inspector of Materials in 1900 and became Assistant to the Divisional Locomotive Superintendent in Paddington four years later.

Further promotions followed, first in 1912 when Churchward appointed him as Assistant Works Manager at Swindon Works, then in 1920 to Works Manager and finally in 1922 when he became principal assistant to the new Chief Mechanical Engineer of the GWR, Charles Collett. His time spent working under Churchward and Collett was to have a great influence on Stanier's later work for the LMS, where he further developed many of the excellent features of GWR locomotive design.

Meanwhile, at the London Midland & Scottish Railway, Sir Henry Fowler was struggling with the development of both heavy freight and passenger locomotive designs for that company. On Fowler's retirement in 1932, William Stanier joined the LMS as their Chief Mechanical Engineer and set about reorganising and standardising the company's rather motley collection of locomotive designs. His designs included the famous 'Black Five' 4-6-0, of which 841 were built, the 'Jubilee' Class

> In the years between 1932 and 1947 over 2,000 Stanier-designed locomotives were built for the LMS, using well tried GWR features such as the tapered boiler and superheating along with Stanier's own development of the Walschaerts valve gear.

4-6-0, of which 190 were built, and the '8F' 2-8-0, of which 776 were built. All of these locomotives provided the backbone of motive power for the LMS and its successor, British Railways (London Midland Region), until the end of steam traction in Britain in 1968. However, Stanier's most famous locomotive designs were the powerful 'Princess' and 'Coronation' Class 4-6-2s, which were the mainstay of the Euston to Glasgow passenger expresses for 30 years.

Stanier was knighted in 1943 and, when he retired as CME of the LMS in 1944, was also elected a Fellow of the Royal Society. He died in Rickmansworth, Hertfordshire, on 27 September 1965.

*Stanier 'Coronation' Class 4-6-2
No. 46225* Duchess of Gloucester,
departing from Carlisle, September 1963

Stanier 'Princess Royal' Class 4-6-2 No. 46207
Princess Arthur of Connaught, *July 1952*

Although Stanier is best known for his steam locomotive designs, he also saw the future for diesel-electric power and was responsible for introducing the forerunner of the humble diesel shunter so favoured by British Railways. During World War II he was one of only three scientific advisers appointed by the Ministry of Production, and was also President of the Institute of Mechanical Engineers.

FAMOUS LOCOMOTIVE ENGINEERS
George Jackson Churchward (1857-1933)

Probably one of the most influential railway engineers of all time, George Jackson Churchward was born into a farming family in Stoke Gabriel, Devon, on 31 January 1857. Surrounded by the beautiful countryside of the Dart estuary, it is not surprising that he never lost his love for this part of the world and of country pursuits.

At school he excelled in mathematics, and in 1873 he joined the Newton Abbot railway works of the broad gauge South Devon Railway where he was apprenticed to John Wright, the railway's Locomotive Superintendent. In 1876 the South Devon Railway became part of the Great Western Railway and Churchward was transferred to the drawing office at that company's Swindon Works. Here he worked for a brief period under Joseph Armstrong, the son of the GWR's locomotive superintendent. A year later William Dean took over this important post and both Churchward and the young Armstrong were given the task of developing a vacuum automatic braking system. In 1881, impressed with Churchward's work, William Dean promoted him to Assistant Manager in the Carriage and Wagon Works. Churchward's career certainly progressed from here as he became Manager of the C&W Works in 1885, Locomotive Works Manager in 1895 and Principal Assistant to William Dean in 1897.

> Along with his love of railways, fishing and shooting, Churchward, who never married, also had a passion for cars and at an early age had built himself a steam-driven vehicle. Around 1900 he took delivery of a very early petrol-driven car; he used it to attend countryside events not accessible by train.

In the same year, Churchward was unanimously elected as the first Mayor of the new Borough of Swindon. In 1902 he reached the pinnacle of his career when he took over as Locomotive, Carriage and Wagon Superintendent from the ailing William Dean. In 1916 this title was changed to Chief Mechanical Engineer, a position he held until his retirement in 1922.

To reduce both construction and maintenance costs, Churchward set about standardising the GWR's locomotives, borrowing well-tried ideas from French and American locomotive designers. Between 1903 and 1911 his four standard, tapered boiler types, ingenious valve gear and the application of superheating were put to good use in the construction of nine standard locomotive designs. The first of these, the powerful inside-cylinder 'City' Class 4-4-0s, was widely based on a successful American design. He went on to design an even more powerful 4-6-0 known as the 'Star' Class, from which his successor, Charles Collett, developed the famous 'Castle' Class locomotives. His only failure was the unique 4-6-2 'Pacific' No. 111 *The Great Bear* which, although extremely powerful, was much too heavy for most of the GWR's routes and was prone to derailment.

Churchward retired in 1922 and continued to live in the house provided for him by a grateful GWR, Newburn House in Dean Street, Swindon, where he was given the services of a chauffeur, housekeeper and two maids. In his later years he suffered from deafness, and this may well have contributed to his death on the misty morning of 19 December 1933 when he was killed by the Paddington to Fishguard express, hauled by No. 4085 *Berkeley Castle*, as he went to inspect a loose rail connection close to his home. He is buried in Christ Church graveyard in Swindon Old Town.

Apart from his advanced locomotive designs, Churchward also designed revolutionary new coaching stock for the GWR and was responsible for the building of the 'A' erecting shop at Swindon Works.

FASTER AND FASTER
The story of *Mallard*'s epic record-breaking run

During the 1920s and 1930s, fierce competition between publicity-seeking railway companies led to a rash of speed record attempts. In Britain, there was rivalry between the London Midland & Scottish Railway (LMS) and the London & North Eastern Railway (LNER). Wind-cheating streamlined casings were *de rigeur* on the powerful 'Pacific' locomotives, and by 1935 the LNER 'A4' Class 'Pacific' *Silver Link* reached 112.5mph. Not to be outdone, the LMS 'Pacific' *Coronation* achieved 114mph just south of Crewe in 1937. However, the all-time world record for steam locomotives was achieved by the LNER on 3 July 1938 with Sir Nigel Gresley's 'A4' Class 'Pacific' No. 4468 *Mallard*.

Designed for running regularly at over 100mph, the three-cylinder design and 6ft 8in driving wheels of Gresley's streamlined 'A4' Class 'Pacifics' were ideally suited for this record-breaking attempt. Crewed by driver Joseph Duddington and fireman Thomas Bray, the 165-ton *Mallard*, along with seven coaches including a dynamometer car together weighing a further 240 tons, accelerated to a speed of 126mph on a downhill stretch of Stoke Bank between Little Bytham and Essendine. Sadly, during the speed record attempt, *Mallard* suffered from an overheated middle big end bearing and was forced to struggle back to Doncaster Works for repair.

Later claims by American railroads that they had exceeded *Mallard*'s officially recorded speed were never substantiated, so the British locomotive still retains its place as the fastest steam locomotive in the world.

Mallard hauled express trains on the East Coast Main Line between King's Cross and Edinburgh until 1963 when she was withdrawn from service. She can be seen today at the National Railway Museum in York.

British Rail Speed Records

DATE	LOCOMOTIVE	LOCATION	RAILWAY COMPANY	SPEED (MPH)	TRACTION TYPE
8 Oct 1829	*Rocket*	Rainhill	Liverpool & Manchester	29.1	steam
15 Sep 1830	*Northumbrian*	Between Parkside and Eccles	Liverpool & Manchester	36	steam
13 Nov 1839	*Lucifer*	Madeley Bank	Grand Junction	56.7	steam
1 Jun 1846	*Great Western*	Nr Wootton Bassett	Great Western	74.5	steam
11 May 1848	*Great Britain*	Nr Wootton Bassett	Great Western	78	steam
Jun 1854	No. 41	Wellington Bank	Bristol & Exeter	81.8	steam
Mar 1897	No. 117	Between Melton Mowbray and Nottingham	Midland	90	steam
9 May 1904	*City of Truro*	Wellington Bank	Great Western	100	steam
5 Mar 1935	*Papyrus*	Stoke Bank	London & North Eastern	108	steam
27 Sep 1935	*Silver Link*	Stoke Bank	London & North Eastern	112.5	steam
27 Jun 1937	*Coronation*	South of Crewe	London, Midland & Scottish	114	steam
3 Jul 1938	*Mallard*	Stoke Bank	London & North Eastern	126	steam
12 Jun 1973	Prototype HST	Between Northallerton and Thirsk	British Rail	143.2	diesel
20 Dec 1979	APT-P	Between Beattock and Gretna	British Rail	162.2	electric
1 Nov 1987	HST	Between Darlington and York	British Rail	148.4	diesel
17 Sep 1989	Class 91 No. 91010	Stoke Bank	British Rail	162	electric
30 Jul 2003	Class 373 set 3313/14	Channel Tunnel Rail Link section 1	Eurostar	208	electric

THE LAST MAIN LINE
The story of the Great Central Railway

The last main line to be built into London, the Great Central Railway had its roots in a much smaller company, the Manchester, Sheffield & Lincolnshire Railway. The MS&LR had existed since 1847 when it was formed by the amalgamation of four railway companies and the Grimsby Docks Company. Its purpose was to improve communications across the Pennines between the important northern industrial centres of Manchester and Sheffield and the fast-growing port of Grimsby.

The MS&LR, under its ambitious General Manager and, later, Chairman, Edward Watkin soon flourished and expanded its territory through takeovers and the arrangement of joint running rights with other railways in the region. Up to that point, despite intense competition from its larger rivals, the MS&LR, a major coal carrier, was thriving. However, Edward Watkins was never a man to sit on his laurels and, as part of his dream to build a railway tunnel under the English Channel, planned further expansion southwards to London.

The new railway, from Annesley in Nottinghamshire to a new London terminus at Marylebone, would transform his company from a regional player into a major north-south strategic route that would compete head on with giants such as the Midland Railway and the Great Northern Railway. One section of the line, southward from Quainton Road in Buckinghamshire to Harrow, was to be jointly run with the Metropolitan Railway, of which Edward Watkin was also Chairman, which had already started operating services on this route in 1892.

The MS&LR obtained parliamentary approval for the London Extension, as it was then known, in 1893 and the following year, to crown his grand dream, Watkin changed the name of his company to the Great Central Railway. Work started on the construction of the 92-mile line in 1895 and it was opened for passenger traffic on 15 March 1899. The line was designed for fast traffic with a continental loading gauge and no level crossings.

Watkins retired as Chairman of the Great Central in 1899 and his place was taken by Alexander Henderson. Sam Fay took over as General Manager in 1902 and, in the same year, John Robinson was appointed Chief Mechanical Engineer. The headquarters of the company moved to Marylebone in 1905. Robinson was a very able locomotive and rolling stock designer and soon the company was living up to its publicity for 'Rapid Travel in Luxury'. Despite this, passenger traffic never lived up to expectations, although the railway did achieve much success as a freight carrier. In the 1923 Grouping, the Great Central became part of the new London & North Eastern Railway and, on nationalisation in 1948, was allocated to the Eastern Region of British Railways.

The Great Central's fortunes took a severe downturn in 1960 when it was transferred to the Midland Region of BR. Marylebone to Manchester expresses were withdrawn and other services were placed in the hands of worn-out steam locomotives. At a time when railway rationalisation and full scale closures were becoming a reality, the duplication of north-south routes into London soon brought about the Great Central's demise. Through freight services were withdrawn on 14 June 1965 and the railway closed as a through route completely on 3 September 1966. Apart from the suburban services from Marylebone to Aylesbury and a short-lived section that was retained for passenger traffic between Rugby Central and Nottingham, the Great Central ceased to exist.

FAMOUS LOCOMOTIVE DESIGNERS
O. V. Bulleid (1882-1970)

Oliver Vaughan Snell Bulleid was born in Invercargill in the South Island of New Zealand on 19 September 1882. His parents had previously emigrated from Britain but after the death of his father, William Bulleid, the seven year-old Oliver returned to Britain with his mother. On completing his education he began an apprenticeship in 1900 with the Great Northern Railway at its Doncaster Works.

Under the watchful eye of the railway's Chief Mechanical Engineer, H. A. Ivatt, Bulleid became assistant to the GNR Locomotive Running Superintendent in 1904 and a year later was promoted to manager of the works. At the age of 26 he moved to Paris where he worked as a test engineer for the Westinghouse Electric Corporation in its brake and signal division, later becoming chief draughtsman and assistant works manager. At this time Bulleid also married Marjorie Ivatt, the daughter of his former boss at Doncaster.

Bulleid returned to Britain in 1910, where he worked for the Board of Trade for two years before rejoining the Great Northern Railway as assistant to its new Chief Mechanical Engineer, Nigel Gresley. Following service in World War I, Bulleid was promoted to manage the GNR's Carriage and Wagon Works before returning to Doncaster in 1923 as Gresley's assistant in the new London & North Eastern Railway. Under Gresley, Bulleid worked on the development of many ground-breaking designs including the Class 'U1' 2-8-0+0-8-2 Garratt and the Class 'P1' and 'P2' 2-8-0 locomotive types.

*Rebuilt 'Merchant Navy' Class 4-6-2
No. 35029 Ellerman Lines, 1964*

In 1937, he was appointed Chief Mechanical Engineer of the Southern Railway following the retirement of Richard Maunsell. This was during a period when that railway was forging ahead with an expensive electrification programme, and spending on new steam locomotive development had been severely restricted.

However, there existed a pressing need for more powerful and modern motive power for its non-electrified lines and Bulleid, despite restrictions imposed during the early years of World War II, had by 1941 produced a new class of innovative steam locomotives. Employing the most up-to-date technology, such as

> Sadly, Bulleid, who was a devout Catholic, lost his son, Hugh, in a cycling accident in 1938 and this terrible tragedy weighed heavily on him for the rest of his life.

high boiler pressure, welded fireboxes, chain-activated and oil-bathed valve gears and disc wheel centres, Bulleid's first major locomotive type, the air-smoothed 'Merchant Navy' Class 4-6-2, was way ahead of the competition. It was soon followed by the more lightweight 'West Country'/'Battle of Britain' Class 4-6-2 and the utilitarian Class 'Q1' 0-6-0 freight engine.

In 1949 Bulleid was appointed Chief Mechanical Engineer for Coras Iompair Eireann (Irish Railways) where he was responsible for the modernisation of that country's antiquated rail system, the early introduction of diesel locomotives and the development of an unusual, but unsuccessful, turf-burning locomotive. He retired from CIE in 1958 and lived in Devon for some years until a deterioration in his health led him to move to the warmer climate of Malta, where he died on 25 April 1970.

> In addition to his ground-breaking steam locomotive designs, Bulleid also went on to introduce improved electric rolling stock, the prototype 'Leader' locomotive powered by steam-operated power bogies, and was a pioneer in the design of main line diesel-electric locomotives.

WARSHIPS AND WESTERNS
The story of the Western Region's short-lived love
affair with diesel-hydraulic transmission

The British Railways' Modernisation Plan of 1955 spelt the end of steam locomotive haulage in this country. Before prototype testing could be properly evaluated, nearly 3,000 main line diesel locomotives of many different non-standard types had been ordered by the British Transport Commission from manufacturers, including British Railways themselves, up and down the country. Most of these locomotives were of the diesel-electric type but the Western Region, still retaining some autonomy left over from the days of Churchward and Collett, decided to favour diesel-hydraulic transmission.

Following the American example, all regions of British Railways, apart from the Western Region, opted for diesel-electric locomotives. The Western Region, however, was favourably impressed with the reliability and performance of the German lightweight diesel-hydraulic locomotives that had been operating successfully on the Deutsche Bundesbahn since 1953. The decision to go hydraulic was made and orders were placed in 1956 to build a British version of the German V200 locomotive using German engines and transmission made under licence.

Briefly, diesel-electrics are locomotives that have a diesel engine that drives a generator. The electric power produced from the generator is then used to power the wheels via electric motors. In a diesel-hydraulic locomotive, the power from the diesel engine is transmitted to the wheels via hydraulic transmission through a torque converter.

The first to be ordered were the five Type 4 A1A-A1A 'Warships', numbered D600-D604, built by the North British Locomotive Company at its Queen's Park Works in Glasgow. These entered service between January 1958 and

January 1959. They were soon employed on main line express services between Paddington and the West Country, but poor reliability, high maintenance costs and incompatibility due to a non-standard design led to their demise. Based for most of their short lives at Plymouth Laira depot, they were relegated to hauling china clay trains in Cornwall. All five locomotives were withdrawn in December 1967 and subsequently scrapped. None of this type was preserved.

There then followed two batches of Type 4 B-B 'Warship' locomotives numbered D800–D870. The first batch, later known as Class 42, numbered D800–D832 and D866–D870, were built at Swindon with deliveries commencing in 1958. The second batch, D833–D865, later known as Class 43, were built by the North British Locomotive Company in Glasgow and delivered from 1960.

Although much more successful than their D600 predecessors, both classes also suffered from poor reliability and high running costs, but for some years they were the mainstay of motive power on main line trains from Paddington to the West Country. The first withdrawals of Class 42 locomotives began in August 1968 and the first Class 43 was withdrawn in March 1969. The final withdrawals took place in December 1972. Two Class 42s have been preserved.

First introduced in January 1959, the D6300 class was never popular and suffered from engine, transmission and train heating faults. Spares became hard to obtain as the North British Locomotive Company went out of business, and members of the class were cannibalised to keep the others running.

The next batch of diesel-hydraulics ordered were the 58 Type 2 B-B D6300 class, otherwise known as 'Baby Warships'. Designed for use on branch lines, they were built by the North British Locomotive Company. Any weight savings that should have been gained by using diesel-hydraulic transmission were completely outweighed by the heavyweight chassis that was built to carry a diesel-electric setup. The first withdrawals began in December 1967 with the last three finally retiring in January 1972. None of this type was preserved.

Introduced in 1961, the Type 3 B-B D7000 'Hymeks' were certainly a vast improvement on the disastrous D6300 Class. A total of 101 were built by Beyer Peacock at its Gorton Works in Manchester. Characterised by their stylish body, colour scheme and raised cast aluminium running numbers, they were soon in use on passenger and freight trains across

Preserved D7017 at Minehead in 1979

the region. After initially suffering from coolant and transmission problems, the class eventually became the most reliable type of diesel-hydraulic used by the Western Region. Withdrawals began in September 1971, with the final members lasting until March 1975. Four members of the class have been preserved.

The final batch of main line diesel-hydraulics to be delivered to the Western Region were the 74 elegant and stylish members of the Type 4 C-C 'Western' Class. Later reclassified as Class 52, they were first introduced at the end of 1961; numbers D1000–D1036 were built at Swindon and D1037–D1073 at Crewe. More powerful than the 'Warship' Class, they were soon in charge of the Western Region's main line expresses. Fitted with two diesel engines, the class suffered from inherent design, transmission and train heating faults and, more importantly, were, as with the other types of WR diesel-hydraulics, of a non-standard design compared to the rest of the BR network. Due for replacement by the Inter-City 125 sets, the first members of

'Western' swansong: Class 52 D1023 Western Fusilier, 1976

the class were withdrawn in May 1973, with the final withdrawals taking place in February 1977. Seven members of the class were purchased privately for restoration.

The final, and least well known, type of diesel-hydraulic locomotives to be ordered were the 56 Type 1 0-6-0 D9500 Class shunting and short trip engines. Later classified as Class 14, they were built at Swindon between 1964 and 1965 and had a relatively short working life with BR. First withdrawals began in March 1968 but many members found their way to industrial railways, such as those run by British Steel and the National Coal Board. Three members of the class were later regauged and exported to Spain. Eight members of the class have been preserved.

So ended the Western Region's love affair with diesel-hydraulics! Taxpayers' money that was spent on this short-sighted, short-lived and selfish exercise would have been better directed towards the electrification of the main lines to the West Country and South Wales. So much for autonomy!

Type 4 'Warship' D869 Zest hauling the down 'Torbay Express', 1962

Type 4 'Warship' D858 Valorous races out of Mill Lane tunnel, near Box, 1963

DR BEECHING, I PRESUME!
The story of the destruction of Britain's railways

Introduced by a Conservative government, the 1962 Transport Act did away with the bureaucratic British Transport Commission and gave British Railways complete autonomy as an independent public corporation for the first time since its formation in 1948. Taking effect on 1 January 1963, the new British Railways Board, chaired by former BTC Chairman Richard Beeching, was faced with the huge problem of ever-increasing railway deficits. A constant drain on the public purse since nationalisation in 1948, Britain's railways were struggling to survive as more and more people and goods were taking to the roads. Even before the Beeching era, about 3,000 miles of uneconomic lines had been closed since nationalisation. Despite this, and the implementation of the 1955 Modernisation Plan, in which regional autonomy had destroyed any chance of standardisation and subsequent reduction in running costs, vast amounts of public money were still being used to shore up what was basically an antiquated and overmanned railway system.

Prior to his appointment as Chairman of the British Railways Board, Richard Beeching had been a member of the Stedeford Committee, an advisory group set up in 1960 by the then Conservative Transport Minister, Ernest Marples, to report on the state of Britain's

It was no coincidence when Marples appointed Beeching as Chairman of the British Railways Board in 1963 – the former already owned a two-thirds share in a major road-building company and the latter wanted to close a third of the railways!

transport system and make recommendations for its improvement. Although Beeching proposed wholesale railway closures, the report was not published. As Chairman, however, Beeching wasted little time in producing his report, entitled *The Reshaping of British Railways*. The first part of his report, which was seized on by Conservative politicians, proposed closing 6,000 miles of

The former Didcot, Newbury and
Southampton Railway, at Whitchurch

The remains of Rugby Central Station; the former Great
Central Railway Station, which closed in 1969

uneconomic rural and cross-country routes, reducing staff by 200,000, closing
2,300 stations, reducing locomotive numbers by 9,000 and scrapping 16,000
carriages and 450,000 freight wagons. The second part of his report proposed
spending large amounts of taxpayers money on modernising and streamlining
the rest of the railways.

The Conservative government approved the first part of Beeching's report,
and branch line closures and the wholesale scrapping of steam engines
reached a peak by 1964. It continued for some years, even under a new
Labour government, which had pledged to halt the cuts. The more positive
side of Beeching's report was never fully implemented and this legacy of under
investment by governments is still evident on Britain's railways today.

By August 1968, all steam traction (apart from three narrow gauge
locomotives on the state-owned Vale of Rheidol Railway) had gone from
British Railways and 3,432 route miles closed. Closures, albeit at a much
slower rate, continued until 1974 when the system stabilised to more or less
what exists today. Beeching was made a life peer in 1965. He died in 1985.

ON SHED, 7 APRIL 1963
The story of a long day out

On Sunday 7 April 1963, the Warwickshire Railway Society organised a coach trip to visit nearly every shed and sub-shed in the South Wales valleys. Sadly, we ran out of time and were unable to visit 88E Abercynon – something that I have always regretted! However, here is a taster of what we saw on that day. As it was a Sunday, nearly every locomotive was on shed. For a full story of this exhausting trip, please see pages 136–8.

88L Cardiff East Dock

3642, 8484, 5942 *Doldowlod Hall*, 5015 *Kingswear Castle*, 5261, 6635, 3804, 3823, 5096 *Bridgwater Castle*, 4633, 4953 *Pitchford Hall*, 4080 *Powderham Castle*, 5074 *Hampden*, 9651, 7303, 3841, 6877 *Llanfair Grange*, 48424, 5749, 6935 *Browsholme Hall*, 9629, 8425, 8748, 8452, 3862, 5220, 5937 *Stanford Hall*, 5225, 5051 *Earl Bathurst*, 5043 *Earl of Mount Edgcumbe*, 6345, 5369, 7315, 6876 *Kingsland Grange*, 1028 *County of Warwick*, 2895, 6995 *Benthall Hall*, 6987 *Shervington Hall*, 5224, 9426, 5014 *Goodrich Castle*, 1000 *County of Middlesex*, 6957 *Norcliffe Hall*, 6939 *Calveley Hall*

88B Radyr

PWM 651, 4213, 5677, 6638, 6682, 6669, 4289, 6607, 5625, 6612, 6621, 5683, D6743, 5635, 3672, 6624, 3409, 3405, 7250, 3402, 3664, D3267, 9480, 5654, 3796, 3681, 8497, 6665, 6672, 6648, 6689, 6637, 6659, 3406, 4637, 6608, 8469, 6656, 9472, 3400, 3401, 6660, 8479, 6684, 5608, 3403, 7252, 4177, 5651, 4160, 5697, 5611, D3423

88C Barry

4618, 3727, 3689, 8466, 5621, 9425, 6696, 7231, 5643, 7202, 5668, 6643, 7208, 3615, 7221, 4667, 3710, 5653, 9794, 3668, 6619, 8728, 5637, 6655, 6650, 6697, 5689, 8471

Woodham's Scrap Yard, Barry

5547, 5182, 9445, 9449, 9499, 7723, 8419, 5510, 9462, 5558, 7722, 9468, 5794, 5557, 5552, 5553, 5542, 5538, 5572, 5539, 4566, 5521, 4561, 5193,

4588, 5532, 5526, 6023 *King Edward II*,
6024 *King Edward I*, 9491, 5422

88G Llantrisant

5248, 6639, 9778, 6670, 4620, 3612,
3661, 4674, 3644, 3680, 6600, 4267

88H Tondu

4121, 9466, 4251, 9678, 3756, 6435,
6676, 9780, 8712, 4243, 9609, 4222,
1422, 4263, 4228, 5243, 9660, 6419,
4669, 3648, 4247, 4262, 5690, 3616,
5208, 4273, 3738, 9649, 4663, 4684,
4269, 4218, 7737, 6431, 6410

Neath (N&B)
sub-shed of 87A Neath

9777, 9734, 4252, 3768, 4699, 4275,
3761, 4660, 3731, 3600, 3693

Glyn Neath
sub-shed of 87A Neath

5221, 5222, 6649, 3766, 9786

88F Treherbert

5669, 5694, 6654, 5684, 5676, 5678,
5674, 5688, 5693, 5695, 5665

Ferndale
sub-shed of 88F Treherbert

5607, 6657, 6699, 5613, 5672, 6614

Dowlais Cae Harris,
sub-shed of 88D Merthyr

5687, 5618, 5681, 5696, 5605

Rhymney
sub-shed of 88D Merthyr

5645, 6603, 5666, 5610, 5671, 5634,
5650, 5655, 5660, 5622, 5662

FAIR EXCHANGE
The story of locomotive exchanges

In the days before nationalisation, Britain's railway companies often tested their locomotives against those of their rivals. Hauling similar loads along the same demanding route, the performance of these engines could be measured against each other and the outcome was quite often surprising.

The 1925 exchanges

Probably one of the most famous of these locomotive exchanges took place in April 1925 when the Great Western Railway's latest design, the 'Castle' Class 4-6-0, was tested against the much larger London & North Eastern Railway's Class 'A3' 4-6-2. During the trials GWR No. 4079 *Pendennis Castle* and LNER No. 2545 *Diamond Jubilee* were tested to the limit first by hauling heavy trains on the East Coast main line out of King's Cross. While the 'Castle' performed faultlessly, the 'A3' lost time on several of its journeys even though it was performing on its home ground – much to the chagrin of the LNER bosses!

Similar tests were conducted on the GWR main line from Paddington to Plymouth, and the 'Castle', this time pitted against 'A3' Class *Victor Wild*, again came out on top – not only was the 'Castle' 15 minutes faster than the 'A3' on both the outward and return journeys but it also used considerably less coal. The GWR had proved once and for all that its locomotive design was far superior to that of its rivals.

The 1948 exchanges

When the 'Big Four' railway companies were nationalised on 1 January 1948 the newly formed British Railways was faced with the mammoth problem of taking over thousands of non-standard steam locomotives, many of them well past their 'sell-by date'. To overcome this, BR planned to build a completely new range of standard steam locomotives that would incorporate all of the best design features from the locomotive stock of the 'Big Four'. Before they could proceed with the building programme, a series of locomotive exchanges were made between four express passenger classes and four mixed traffic classes to ascertain the relative merits of each one. They all had to haul the same weight along designated routes using the same, Yorkshire, coal.

Express passenger locomotive trials

The routes used for the trials were as follows:

> London Euston to Carlisle
> London Paddington to Plymouth
> London Waterloo to Exeter
> London Kings Cross to Leeds

For the express passenger classes, the following type of locomotives were used, each one being required to haul the same weight train along each of the designated routes and burning the same, Yorkshire, coal:

> LMS – Stanier 'Coronation' Class 4-6-2
> GWR – Collett 'King' Class 4-6-0
> LNER – Gresley Class 'A4' 4-6-2
> SR – Bulleid 'Merchant Navy' Class 4-6-2
> A fifth locomotive class, the LMS Stanier 'Royal
> Scot' Class 4-6-0 was added to the list at the last moment.

It must be remembered that, while these locomotives were designed to haul expresses on their own home ground, some of them were not particularly well suited for the testing uphill sections that they encountered in the trials.

The results were a mixed bag with, surprisingly, the smaller and less powerful 'Royal Scot' probably giving the best overall performance, particularly with its exhilarating run from Taunton to Paddington where it arrived over 16 minutes ahead of schedule. The 'King' probably suffered most because it had to burn Yorkshire coal instead of the South Wales coal that it was designed to use.

Apart from one amazing performance between Salisbury and Waterloo, the 'Duchess', too, did not fare too well. The 'Merchant Navy' put in some worthy runs on the formidable section between Penrith and Carlisle but paid for this performance with very high oil and coal consumption. Finally, the 'A4', despite some mechanical problems, probably gave the best performance out of the four larger locos, turning in a scintillating run on the former GWR main line.

While not perfect, these trials provided much useful data, some of which was incorporated into the design of the new Standard 'Britannia' Class 4-6-2s introduced by British Railways in 1951.

Mixed traffic locomotive exchanges

The routes used for the trials were as follows:

> London St Pancras to Manchester
> Exeter to Bristol
> London Marylebone to Manchester
> Perth to Inverness

For the mixed traffic classes the following type of locomotives were used and, as before, each one was required to haul the same weight train along each of the designated routes and burning the same, Yorkshire, coal:

LMS Stanier Class '5'
(the 'Black Five') at Leeds City

LMS – Stanier 'Black 5' 4-6-0
GWR– Collett 'Hall' Class 4-6-0
LNER – Thompson Class 'B1' 4-6-0
SR – Bulleid 'West Country' Class 4-6-2

Unlike the mixed bag of results with the express locomotives there was one clear winner from these trials. Without a doubt, the 'West Country' excelled on all of the routes giving extremely impressive performances on even the most demanding sections. Both the 'Hall' and 'B1' performed well in a workmanlike way but, surprisingly, the 'Black 5' turned in very poor times.

One eminent railway historian and recorder of locomotive performances of that time, Cecil J. Allen, was shocked that the highly regarded 'Black 5', which had already put in such sterling work for the LMS, had failed so miserably! It appeared that the problem probably didn't lie with the locomotive at all but with the driver and fireman who had obviously lost the plot and decided to break the world record for the least amount of fuel consumed in the trials!

Although the 'West Country' was the winner, its heavy consumption of fuel let it down and it was the already tried-and-tested 'Black 5' that was used as the blueprint for the design of the new Standard 'Class 5' 4-6-0s, introduced by British Railways in 1951. As with the 'Black 5', these new locomotives gave sterling service on British Railways up until the end of steam in 1968.

Fortunately, examples of all of the types of locomotives used in the exchanges have been preserved, as follows: two LMS 'Coronation' Class 4-6-2s; three GWR 'King' Class 4-6-0s; six LNER 'A4' Class 4-6-2s; two SR 'Merchant Navy' Class 4-6-2s; two LMS 'Royal Scot' 4-6-0s; five LMS 'Black Five' 4-6-0s; ten GWR 'Hall' Class 4-6-0s; two LNER 'B1' Class 4-6-0s; and 20 SR 'West Country'/'Battle of Britain' Class 4-6-2s.

SMALL IS BEAUTIFUL
The story of the world's smallest public railway

The world's smallest public railway, the Romney, Hythe & Dymchurch Railway, was conceived by two wealthy men, Captain Jack Howey and Count Louis Zborowski, in the 1920s.

Both men had a love of motor racing and miniature railways and Howey had already gained experience in the operation of a 15in gauge line in the grounds of his estate, Staughton Manor, in Huntingdonshire.

Romney, Hythe & Dymchurch Railway No. 3 Southern Maid *on the turntable at Hythe in 1969*

They were initially interested in buying the Ravenglass & Eskdale Railway in the Lake District where they planned to rebuild the narrow gauge line as a 15in gauge line. This plan fell through but two, one-third scale LNER steam engines, designed by Henry Greenly, had already been ordered from Davey Paxman of Colchester at a cost of £1,600 each. Meanwhile Count Zborowski was tragically killed in a motor racing accident in the Italian Grand Prix at Monza, and Howey teamed up with Greenly to look for a new location for the railway.

With the growing popularity of the beaches between Hythe and new Romney and the lack of

> The terminus at Hythe boasts a roof covering its three platforms. During peak periods trains run from here every 45 minutes, at speeds of up to 25mph. Services operate most weekends throughout the year, except January, with a full service between April and October.

suitable transport to serve the holidaymakers, the pair finally chose Romney Marsh in Kent as the location for their miniature railway. No expense was spared to produce an accurate, one-third scale, working miniature of a main line railway. The line was double track and signalled, engines were replicas of LNER and Canadian express locomotives, and passengers were carried in bogie carriages.

The first 8-mile section of the line, from Hythe to New Romney, was opened on 16 July 1927 and the then Duke of York, later to become King George VI, had the honour of driving the first train. A year later the line was extended a further 5½ miles westward to Dungeness lighthouse, where the line makes a complete loop. Further steam locomotives were built and during the pre-war years the line became very popular with holidaymakers.

Located on the south coast of England, the railway also played its part in the defence of Britain during World War II. An armoured train was built, complete with machine guns, and the line transported materials for Operation Pluto (Pipe Line Under The Ocean) in the days before the D-Day landings. The railway was reopened to the public in 1947 with Laurel and Hardy performing the ceremony.

The period after the war brought mixed fortunes for the little railway and, with passenger numbers down, losses mounted after Howey's death in 1963 until the line was put up for sale in 1968. The new owners fared little better and it seemed that the line might well close until it was rescued in 1973 by a consortium headed by Sir William MacAlpine.

Since then, the line has been restored to its former glory and now boasts 11 steam locomotives, including the two original 1925 locos, *Green Goddess* and *Northern Chief*, and two diesels that are used to operate a regular school train during term time. Rolling stock consists of over 65 assorted coaches, including a unique buffet observation car and a royal saloon. The headquarters of the line is at New Romney where there is a large engine shed, turntable and workshop.

UP IN THE CLOUDS
The story of the Snowdon Mountain Railway

Although other mountain railways were proposed on mainland Britain at the end of the 19th century, the only one to be built, the Snowdon Mountain Railway, was opened on 6 April 1896. Operating on the Swiss Abt system, the 2ft 7½in gauge line climbs from the terminus at Llanberis for 4½ miles on gradients as steep as 1 in 5.5 to the summit terminus at an altitude of 3,493ft above sea level.

Motive power is provided by Swiss-built 0-4-2T steam and diesel locomotives, which push their coach up the mountain using a series of cogs and a double rack laid between the track. This rack-and-pinion system also provides braking on the downward journey.

The steam locomotives, two of which date from 1895, have a forward-tilted firebox and boiler so that water levels remain fairly horizontal on the steep gradient. To supplement the ageing steam locomotives, four 320hp diesel locomotives and three diesel-electric railcars were delivered to the line between 1986 and 1995.

The summit station building was originally built as a restaurant and designed in the 1930s by the architect responsible for the famous village of Portmeirion, Clough Williams-Ellis. This building was demolished in 2006 to make way for a more modern structure.

Construction began in 1894 and was completed in February 1896 at a cost of £76,000. The line was opened to the public on Easter Monday, 6 April. However, this happy event turned into a disaster when locomotive No. 1 *Ladas* became derailed on its downward journey from the summit with the first official train. The engine was at the front of the train and the two carriages, which were not coupled to it, were able to stop with their own brakes. Just before the engine hurtled down the mountainside, the driver and fireman managed to jump out of the cab, but a passenger in one of the carriages who did likewise was killed. The following train pulled by locomotive No. 2 *Enid* also became derailed at the same spot and ran into the carriages of the first train – fortunately nobody else was killed.

Soon after the opening day accident, the Board of Trade halted all services on the line and set up a Board of Enquiry. It found that the accident had been caused by settlement of the ground under the track and recommended improvements to the rack rail and a reduction of the maximum load for locomotives. The line was finally reopened on 9 April 1897 and has been operating without any major incident ever since.

Snowdon Mountain Railway No. 8 Enid restarting from Clogwyn station with a train for the summit, September 1971

Two trains wait in Clogwyn station while another descends to Llanberis, September 1971

Weather permitting, trains currently operate from mid-March to the first week of November. Including stops, the train takes an hour to climb to the summit, with an average speed of 5mph.

WE NEVER CLOSED!
The story of the Talyllyn Railway – the world's first preserved railway

Opened in 1865 to carry slate from the Bryn Eglwys quarries to the harbour at Towyn, this 7-mile-long, 2ft 3in narrow gauge line became the first railway in the world to be saved from closure and preserved. In 1911 both the quarries and railway were purchased by the local MP for Merioneth, Sir Haydn Jones, who also developed the line as a tourist attraction. Between the wars, slate traffic dwindled and passenger traffic was lost to competing buses, so by 1946, when the quarries closed, the line was in a sad state of repair. Somehow, passenger trains still ran in the summer months along the grass-covered tracks but when Sir Haydn Jones died in 1950, it seemed certain that the line would finally close.

A group of railway enthusiasts, led by L.T.C. Rolt amongst others, had already met Sir Haydn before he died, with a view to saving the line from closure. On his death, the non-profit-making Talyllyn Railway Preservation Society was formed to take over the running of the line.

Faced with the run-down state of the line, locomotives and rolling stock, the volunteers had to look further afield before they could open the line for the 1951 summer season. A few miles away, the narrow gauge Corris Railway had ceased to operate in 1947 and two locomotives, rolling stock and a quantity of rail was purchased from the railways owners, British Railways (Western

In addition to co-founding the Talyllyn Railway Preservation Society in the early 1950s, Lionel Thomas Caswall Rolt (1910–1974) was co-founder of the Inland Waterways Association. He was a prolific author on civil engineering, canals and railways, and lived for many years on a canal narrowboat.

Region), at a knock-down price. Volunteers worked feverishly to get the railway ready for its opening. New track was laid, the sole steam engine still operating, the temperamental 85-year-old *Dolgoch*, was given a boiler examination, overhanging trees along the line side were cut back and new signs erected.

> The Talyllyn Railway now operates a regular steam-hauled passenger service between Towyn Wharf and Nant Gwernol from the end of March to the beginning of November.

Whit Monday, 1951, dawned, the sun shone from a blue sky and the Talyllyn Railway was back in business, operating a limited passenger service between Towyn and Rhydyronen. Watched by Sir Haydn Jones's widow, ancient *Dolgoch* and her train of four-wheeled carriages wheezed out of Wharf Station and up the incline to the first stop at Pendre. The railway had been saved! Much work was still to be done, but those early enthusiasts certainly deserve our thanks in saving this beautiful little line for generations to come.

Double-heading on the Talyllyn Railway, Easter 1972, with No. 6 Douglas *piloting No. 2* Dolgoch

British Standard Gauge Passenger-Carrying Heritage Railways

Alderney Railway
Location: Alderney, Channel Islands
Route: Braye Harbour – Mannez Quarry
Length: 2 miles

Appleby Frodingham Railway
Location: Corus Steel Works, Scunthorpe
Route: Within steel works
Length: 15 miles

Avon Valley Railway
Location: Bitton Station, Willsbridge, Nr Bristol
Route: Bitton – Oldland – Avon Riverside
Length: 3 miles

The Battlefield Line Railway
Location: Shackerstone Railway Station, Shackerstone, Leicestershire
Route: Shackerstone – Shenton
Length: 4¾ miles

Bluebell Railway
Location: Sheffield Park Station, Nr Uckfield, East Sussex
Route: Sheffield Park – Kingscote
Length: 9 miles

Bo'ness & Kinneil Railway
Location: Bo'ness Station, Union Street, Bo'ness, West Lothian
Route: Bo'ness – Manuel Junction
Length: 5 miles

Bodmin & Wenford Railway
Location: Bodmin General Station, Bodmin, Cornwall
Route: Bodmin Parkway – Bodmin General – Boscarne Junction
Length: 6½ miles

Bowes Railway
Location: Springwell Village, Nr Gateshead, Tyne & Wear
Route: Springwell – Black Fell
Length: 2 miles

Caledonian Railway
Location: The Station, 2 Park Road, Brechin, Angus
Route: Brechin – Bridge of Dun
Length: 4 miles

Chasewater Railway
Location: Brownhills Station, Hednesford Road, Brownhills West, Walsall
Route: Brownhills West – Chasetown (Church Street)
Length: 2 miles

Chinnor & Princes Risborough Railway
Location: Chinnor Station, Nr Princes Risborough, Buckinghamshire
Route: Chinnor – Wainhill
Length: 3½ miles

Cholsey & Wallingford Railway
Location: Wallingford Station, Hithercroft Road, Wallingford, Oxfordshire
Route: Cholsey – Wallingford
Length: 2½ miles

Churnet Valley Railway

Location: Cheddleton Station, Station Road, Cheddleton, Staffs
Route: Leek Brook Junction – Cheddleton – Kingsley & Froghall
Length: 5½ miles

Dartmoor Railway

Location: Okehampton Station, Station Road, Okehampton, Devon
Route: Okehampton – Meldon Quarry
Length: 2 miles

Dean Forest Railway

Location: Norchard Railway Centre, Forest Road, Lydney, Gloucestershire
Route: Lydney – Parkend
Length: 4 miles

East Kent Railway

Location: Shepherdswell Station, Shepherdswell, Nr Dover, Kent
Route: Shepherdswell – Eythorne
Length: 2 miles

East Lancashire Railway

Location: Bolton Street Station, Bury, Lancashire
Route: Heywood – Rawtenstall
Length: 9 miles

East Somerset Railway

Location: Cranmore Station, Nr Shepton Mallet, Somerset
Route: Cranmore – Mendip Vale
Length: 2½ miles

Ecclesbourne Valley Railway

Location: Wirksworth Station, Coldwell Street, Wirksworth, Derbyshire
Route: Duffield – Wirksworth
Length: 8½ miles

Embsay & Bolton Abbey Steam Railway

Location: Embsay Station, Embsay, Nr Skipton, Yorkshire
Route: Embsay – Bolton Abbey
Length: 6 miles

Epping Ongar Railway

Location: Station Road, High Street, Ongar, Essex
Route: Epping – Ongar
Length: 6 miles

Foxfield Light Railway

Location: Caverswall Road Station, Blythe Bridge, Stoke-on-Trent, Staffs
Route: Blythe Bridge – Dilhorne Park
Length: 2½ miles

Gloucestershire Warwickshire Railway

Location: The Railway Station, Toddington, Gloucestershire
Route: Toddington – Cheltenham Racecourse
Length: 10 miles

Great Central Railway

Location: Loughborough Central Station, Great Central Road, Loughborough, Leicestershire
Route: Loughborough Central – Leicester North
Length: 8 miles

Gwili Railway

Location: Bronwyth Arms
Route: Bronwydd Arms – Danycoed
Length: 2¼ miles

Isle of Wight Steam Railway

Location: Havenstreet, Isle of Wight
Route: Smallbrook Junction – Wootton
Length: 5 miles

Keighley & Worth Valley Railway

Location: Haworth Station, Nr Keighley, West Yorkshire
Route: Keighley – Oxenhope
Length: 5 miles

Keith & Dufftown Railway

Location: Dufftown Station, Dufftown, Banffshire
Route: Keith – Dufftown
Length: 11 miles

Kent & East Sussex Railway

Location: Tenterden Town Station, Tenterden, Kent
Route: Tenterden Town – Bodiam
Length: 10 miles

Lakeside & Haverthwaite Railway

Location: Haverthwaite Station, Nr Ulverston, Cumbria
Route: Haverthwaite – Lakeside
Length: 3½ miles

Llangollen Railway

Location: Llangollen Station, Abbey Road, Llangollen, Clwyd
Route: Llangollen – Corwen
Length: 10 miles

Mid-Hants Watercress Line

Location: Alresford Station, Alresford, Hampshire
Route: Alresford – Alton
Length: 10 miles

Middleton Railway

Location: The Station, Moor Road, Leeds
Route: Moor Road – Middleton Park
Length: 1¼ miles

Midland Railway Centre

Location: Butterley Station, Nr Ripley, Derbyshire
Route: Hammersmith – Swanick — Ironville
Length: 3½ miles

Nene Valley Railway

Location: Wansford Station, Stibbington, Peterborough, Cambridgeshire
Route: Yarwell Junction – Peterborough
Length: 7½ miles

North Norfolk Railway

Location: Sheringham Station, Sheringham, Norfolk
Route: Sheringham – Holt
Length: 5¼ miles

North Tyneside Steam Railway

Location: Middle Engine Lane, West Chirton, North Shields, Tyne and Wear
Route: Percy Main – Middle Engine Lane
Length: 1¾ miles

North Yorkshire Moors Railway

Location: Pickering Station, Pickering, North Yorks
Route: Pickering – Grosmont – Whitby
Length: 24 miles

Northampton & Lamport Railway

Location: Pitsford & Brampton Station, Pitsford Road, Chapel Brampton, Northampton
Route: Either side of station
Length: ¾ mile

Paignton & Dartmouth Steam Railway

Location: Queen's Park Station, Paignton, Devon
Route: Paignton – Kingswear
Length: 7 miles

Peak Rail

Location: Matlock Station, Matlock, Derbyshire
Route: Matlock Riverside – Rowsley
Length: 3½ miles

Pontypool & Blaenavon Railway

Location: Big Pit Mining Museum, Blaenavon, Gwent
Route: Whistle Inn - Blaenavon
Length: 2 miles

Severn Valley Railway

Location: Railway Station, Bewdley, Worcestershire
Route: Kidderminster Town – Bridgnorth
Length: 16 miles

South Devon Railway

Location: Buckfastleigh Station, Buckfastleigh, Devon
Route: Buckfastleigh – Totnes
Length: 7 miles

Spa Valley Railway

Location: West Station, Royal Tunbridge Wells, Kent
Route: Royal Tunbridge Wells – Eridge
Length: 5½ miles

Strathspey Steam Railway

Location: Aviemore Station, Dalfaber Road, Aviemore, Inverness-shire
Route: Aviemore – Boat of Garten
Length: 5 miles

Swanage Railway 'The Purbeck Line'

Location: Swanage Station, Swanage, Dorset
Route: Swanage – Norden
Length: 6 miles

Swindon & Cricklade Railway

Location: Blunsden Station, Blunsden, Wilts
Route: Blunsden – South Meadow Lane
Length: 1 mile

Tanfield Railway

Location: Marley Hill Engine Shed, Sunniside, Gateshead
Route: East Tanfield – Sunniside
Length: 3 miles

Vale of Glamorgan Railway (Barry Island Railway)

Closed pending move to Garw Valley Railway

West Somerset Railway

Location: The Railway Station, Minehead, Somerset
Route: Minehead – Bishop's Lydeard
Length: 20 miles

120 INTO 4 = THE 'BIG FOUR'
The story of the creation of the 'Big Four' in 1923

By the outbreak of World War I there were 120 separate railway companies operating in Britain and, with a duplication of routes, many of them were competing directly with each other. Losses were mounting and the government of the day wanted to introduce a more efficient and economical working of the railway system. Nationalisation was considered by members of the fledgling Labour Party but there was not enough support for this at the time.

After the war, during which the railways had come under state control, the coalition government, under the premiership of David Lloyd-George, enacted the Railways Act of 1921, which amalgamated these 120 companies into four larger regional companies. Taking effect on 1 January 1923, the Act brought about the formation of the 'Big Four', as they soon became known.

The 'Big Four'
Great Western Railway (GWR)
London, Midland & Scottish Railway (LMS)
London & North Eastern Railway (LNER)
Southern Railway (SR)

The pre-1923 railway companies that constituted the 'Big Four' were as follows:

Great Western Railway constituent companies
(total mileage 3,566 miles):
Great Western Railway
Cambrian Railways
Taff Vale Railway
Barry Railway
Rhymney Railway

Cardiff Railway
Alexandra Docks & Railway

Subsidiary companies within the newly formed GWR included five that still continued to be independently worked (total mileage 169 miles), two that were semi-independent (total mileage 64 miles) and 19 that were originally leased to, or worked by, its constituent companies

LMS unrebuilt 'Royal Scot' Class 4-6-0 No. 6137 Vesta *near Kenton in the 1930s*

(total mileage 151¼ miles). The GWR also operated one joint line (total mileage 41 miles) with the LNER, 15 joint lines with the LMS (total 247¾ miles) and two with the SR (total 9 miles).

London, Midland & Scottish Railway constituent companies

(total mileage 7,331 miles):
London & North Western Railway
Lancashire & Yorkshire Railway
Furness Railway
Midland Railway
North Staffordshire Railway
Caledonian Railway
Glasgow & South Western Railway
Highland Railway

Subsidiary companies within the newly formed LMS included six that still continued to be independently worked (total mileage 170 miles), and 20 (total mileage 442 miles) that were originally leased to, or worked by, its constituent companies.

The LMS also absorbed three railways in Ireland:

Northern Counties Committee

Dundalk, Newry & Greenore Railway

Joint Midland & Great Northern Railway (Ireland)

The LMS also operated a total of 21 joint lines (total mileage 585¼ miles) with the LNER, 15 joint lines with the GWR (total mileage 247¾ miles), one joint line with the Southern Railway (the Somerset & Dorset Joint Railway – total mileage 105 miles) and one with the Metropolitan District Railway (total mileage 2 miles).

Railways not included in the 'Big Four' Grouping of 1923 included the London Underground lines (total mileage 66 miles), the Liverpool Overhead Railway (6½ miles), the Mersey Railway (4¾ miles) and the Metropolitan Railway (65¾ miles). A total of 18 standard gauge light railways (total mileage 206¾ miles), including those run by Colonel Stephens (see pages 16–17), were excluded, as were 15 narrow gauge light railways (total mileage 101¾ miles).

London & North Eastern Railway constituent companies

(total mileage 6,671¾ miles):

North Eastern Railway

North British Railway

Great Eastern Railway

Great Northern Railway

Great Central Railway

Great North of Scotland Railway

Hull & Barnsley Railway

Subsidiary companies within the newly formed LNER included three that still continued to be independently worked (total mileage 48 miles) and 23 (total mileage 269 miles) that were originally leased to, or worked by, its constituent companies.

Great Northern Railway 4-2-2 No. 774 piloting 2-2-2 No. 872 with the down 'Flying Scotsman' near Hadley Wood in 1898

Great Northern Railway 4-4-2 No. 274 with an up express in 1905

The LNER also operated a total of 21 joint lines (total mileage 585¼ miles) with the LMS, and one (total mileage 41 miles) with the GWR.

Southern Railway constituent companies (total mileage 2,115½ miles):
London & South Western Railway
South Eastern Railway
London, Chatham & Dover Railway
London, Brighton & South Coast Railway

Subsidiary companies within the newly formed SR included four that still continued to be independently worked (total mileage 65½ miles) and 12 (total mileage 128¾ miles) that were originally leased to, or worked by, its constituent companies.

The SR also operated a total of one joint line with the LMS (the Somerset & Dorset Joint Railway – total mileage 105 miles), two with the GWR (total mileage 9 miles), one with the LNER and the Metropolitan District Railway (total mileage 5 miles), and one with the GWR and LMS (total mileage 5¼ miles).

4 INTO 1 = BR
The story of the creation of British Railways in 1948

The idea of nationalising Britain's railways dates back to the early days of the Labour Party. However, although Private Members' Bills were put forward as early as 1906, it wasn't until the Labour Party had a big enough majority in parliament after World War II that this dream became a reality.

For strategic reasons, Britain's railways came under government control during World War I and in 1920 the then Minister of Transport, Sir Eric Geddes, first put forward a serious proposal to nationalise the railways. However, this plan came at the time of a post-war coalition government and sufficient support within Parliament was not forthcoming. Instead, the 1921 Railways Act created four large railway companies out of a previous total of 120 and the 'Big Four' – the GWR, LMS, LNER and SR – were created.

The railways again came under government control during World War II and when the Labour Party were elected with a landslide majority in 1945, they seized the opportunity to create their Socialist dream and nationalise Britain's run-down railways. When it was finally given the green light by Parliament, the 1947 Transport Act created the British Transport Commission to oversee the modernisation and integration of all of Britain's public transport systems. This not only included all but a few minor railways, but also all public road, canal and air transport.

> Despite most freight and passenger traffic still being carried by rail, the Big Four grouping was not a total success and by the beginning of World War II many parts of the system were suffering from lack of investment.

From 1 January 1948 the railways were run by a body called the Railway Executive, which was, in principle, answerable to the BTC. So British Railways was born.

From the outset British Railways had one hand tied behind its back. Even before World War II, railway companies were forced by the government to carry goods at a rate set by a parliamentary tribunal. This common carrier status was continued after nationalisation but no similar price fixing was applied to road transport, which was free to undercut the railway's charges. British Railways' legal liability as a common carrier was not ended until 1956, by which time it was too late as road transport had by then creamed off much of the freight business.

BR Standard 'Britannia' Class 4-6-2 No. 70022 Tornado with 'The Devonian' in August 1955

On formation, British Railways was faced with the enormous task of not only repairing about 20,000 miles of worn-out track and associated infrastructure, but also of modernising and standardising its fleet of over 20,000 steam locomotives, over one million goods wagons and over 55,000 passenger carriages. With a payroll of over half a million workers, the newly formed BR soon placed an enormous burden on the British taxpayer.

British Railways was initially divided into six geographical regions similar to the make-up of the old Big Four railway companies. Although there was some central control, these regions still possessed a large amount of autonomy – a situation that did not lend itself to an integrated rail system or standardisation of equipment. Many of the old practices of the previous Big Four companies still held sway and when the 1955 Modernisation Plan was announced, some regions, in particular the Western Region, went their own way, with disastrous results in later years (see pages 48–51).

The new BR soon went ahead with the standardisation of locomotive types, with 11 classes of successful standard locomotives built between 1951 and 1960. Many non-standard and ageing steam locomotives were scrapped. New passenger carriages and freight wagons were also introduced.

NARROW GAUGE ADVENTURE
The story of Welsh narrow gauge railways

Since the rescue of the Talyllyn Railway by a group of railway enthusiasts in 1951 (see pages 64–65), many other Welsh narrow gauge preservation schemes have emerged and are now amongst the most popular tourist attractions in the principality.

Ffestiniog Railway double Fairlie Merdinn Emrys, 1979

Corris Railway

Opened in 1859 to transport slate from the quarries around Corris to the Cambrian main line at Machynlleth, this 2ft 3in gauge line was originally worked as a horse tramway. Steam locomotives were introduced in 1879 and passenger services in 1883. In 1930 the railway was taken over by the GWR, and passenger traffic ceased a year later. Nationalised on 1 January 1948, the line ceased operating on 20 August of that year when the Afon Dyfi flooded and severely damaged the southern section. Two of the railway's steam locomotives and some goods wagons were purchased by the Talyllyn Railway in 1951 and can still be seen in operation on that railway today.

Formed in 1966, the Corris Railway Society has reopened a section of line, and passenger services, hauled by a new steam locomotive based on an original Corris engine, now operate from Corris to Maespoeth. The Society hopes to extend the line southwards towards Machynlleth.

Ffestiniog Railway

Opened in 1836 as a horse-drawn and gravity tramway to carry slate from the quarries at Blaenau Ffestiniog down to the harbour at Porthmadog, the 1ft 11½in gauge Ffestiniog Railway was converted to steam power in 1865 (see pages 130-1). Passenger services on this independent railway were withdrawn in 1939, but goods traffic continued through to 1946 when the line closed. A preservation group was formed in 1951 and the first section of line from Porthmadog to Boston Lodge was reopened to passengers in 1955. The 13½-mile line was then reopened in stages to Tan-y-Bwlch, Dduallt, finally reaching Blaenau Ffestiniog in 1982.

> Trains run on this scenic line throughout the year with a full service operating between the end of March and early November.

Passengers are carried in Victorian rolling stock hauled by oil-fired steam locomotives, including the unique double Fairlies, all of which have been beautifully restored in the company's Boston Lodge Works.

Vale of Rheidol Railway

Opened in 1902, this 1ft 11¾in gauge line was originally built to serve lead mines, the timber industry and tourism. In 1913 the Vale of Rheidol Railway was taken over by Cambrian Railways, which in turn was absorbed by the Great Western Railway in 1922. While goods traffic had ceased by 1920, the GWR virtually rebuilt the line as a tourist attraction and modernised the locomotives and rolling stock.

Temporarily closed during World War II, the railway was nationalised in 1948 and, after the end of main-line steam in 1968, became the only steam-operated line run by British Railways. It was finally sold by BR in 1989 and the three original steam locomotives converted to oil burning. The company now operates steam-hauled trains along the scenic 11¾-mile line between the months of April and October.

Welsh Highland Railway

The Welsh Highland railway originated as the North Wales Narrow Gauge Railway Company in 1877 and was acquired by the Welsh Highland Railway in 1923. The 22-mile line, the longest in Wales, ran through the heart of Snowdonia from Dinas Junction, south of Caernarfon, to Porthmadog via Beddgelert and the Pass of Aberglaslyn. It was not a commercial success and finally closed in 1937.

In 1964 a preservation group was formed to reopen the line and, after much legal argument, the neighbouring Ffestiniog Railway was finally allowed to take on the rebuilding and operation of the line in 1995. Aided by major lottery funding and EU grants, the first phase of this major project is now complete between Caernarfon and Rhyd Ddu, including the first three miles along the trackbed of the former BR standard gauge line between Caernarfon and Dinas Junction. The southern section to Porthmadog Harbour was completed in 2011, providing a connection with the Ffestiniog Railway and allowing through trains to run between Caernarfon and Blaenau Ffestiniog. Trains, mainly steam-hauled, operate all year round, with a full service between March and mid-November.

Welshpool & Llanfair Railway

One of the first railways built under the 1896 Light Railways Act, the 2ft 6in gauge Welshpool & Llanfair Light Railway opened in 1903 to link farming communities in the Banwy Valley with the market town of Welshpool. It has some of the steepest gradients (1 in 24) on any adhesion railway in Britain and, until closure, the last section of the line ran through the back streets of Welshpool to connect with the town's standard gauge station.

From its opening, the line was operated by Cambrian Railways until

Steam trains on the Welshpool and Llanfair Railway are operated by the line's two original Beyer Peacock engines and rolling stock from many countries around the world. Services operate from the end of March through to the end of October.

absorbed into the GWR in 1923. Passenger traffic ceased in 1931 but goods traffic continued through nationalisation in 1948 until closure by BR in 1956. A preservation group reopened part of the line to passengers in 1963. The line was later reopened as far as Welshpool (Raven Square) where a new terminus was built on the western outskirts of the town.

Bala Lake Railway

This 1ft 11½in gauge railway runs along the trackbed of the former standard gauge Bala & Dolgelly Railway which opened in 1868. Closed by BR in 1965, the present line was opened in the 1970s. Steam and diesel passenger trains operate between April and October along 4½ miles on the eastern shore of Lake Bala between Bala and the original standard gauge station at Llanuwchllyn.

Brecon Mountain Railway

This 1ft 11¾in gauge railway runs for 3½ miles along part of the trackbed of the former Brecon & Merthyr Tydfil Junction Railway, which opened in 1868 and was closed in 1964. Construction of the present line started in 1978 and the first trains ran from Pant to Pontiscill in 1980. The line has since been extended alongside Taf Fechan Reservoir to a temporary terminus at Dol-y-Gaur.

> Steam trains, hauled by former German and American narrow gauge locomotives, run on the Brecon line from mid-February to the end of October.

Llanberis Lake Railway

The 4ft gauge Padarn Railway was opened in 1843 to transport slate from the quarries at Llanberis to Port Dinorwic. Originally a horse-drawn tramway, the line was converted to steam haulage in 1848. The present 1ft 11½in gauge line was opened along two miles of the trackbed of the old Padarn Railway between Llanberis (Gilfach Ddu) and Penllyn in 1972. Since extended to Llanberis Village, passenger services are hauled by diminutive steam locomotives.

A RIGHT ROYAL RAILWAY
The story of Britain's
royal trains

Stanier Class '5' 4-6-0 No. 44902 with the royal train, 1958

The first recorded train journey by royalty occurred on 14 November 1839 when Prince Albert travelled from Slough to Paddington on Brunel's recently opened GWR broad gauge line. Queen Adelaide, the widow of William IV, travelled on the London & Birmingham Railway in 1840 and the company responded by building her own royal carriage, now in the National Railway Museum in York.

The first reigning monarch to travel by train was Queen Victoria when she travelled back to London from Windsor Castle on 13 June 1842. Joining the train at Slough and accompanied by Isambard Kingdom Brunel, she travelled in a purpose-built four-wheeled carriage supplied by the Great Western Railway. The train, hauled by the GWR broad gauge locomotive *Phlegethon*, took 25 minutes for the journey to Paddington.

Following her acquisition of Osborne in the Isle of Wight in 1843 and Balmoral in Scotland in 1848, Victoria became a regular long distance railway traveller, and special trains were supplied for her use by the various railway companies involved. However, her trips were highly disruptive to normal traffic as Victoria disliked speed and her journeys had a maximum 40mph limit.

In later years, Edward VII, who loved travelling at speed, had three new luxurious royal trains built at great expense to himself.

> Many of the royal carriages built during Edward's reign were so comfortable that they continued to be used during the reigns of George V and George VI. Some of these can be seen at the National Railway Museum in York.

The high cost of maintaining and running these trains was met by the royal household, which was even charged by the railway companies for the conveyance of royal pets! A new set of armour-plated royal carriages was built during World War II and these continued in use until a modern set was built to commemorate Elizabeth II's Silver Jubilee in 1977. The current royal train, consisting entirely of eight refurbished Mark III carriages, has been in use since 1986.

Railway companies often nominated specific locomotives for hauling royal trains but the most famous must be GWR 'Castle' Class 4-6-0 No. 4082 *Windsor Castle*. Only a few weeks old, the locomotive hauled the royal train taking King George V from Paddington for a visit to Swindon Works on 28 April 1924.

After his visit, the king drove *Windsor Castle* from the Works to Swindon Station. Commemorative plaques were mounted on the cab side in memory of this event, and the locomotive was consequently used to haul all royal trains on the GWR, including George V's funeral train in 1936.

When George VI died at Sandringham in 1952, *Windsor Castle* was undergoing repair at Swindon Works and locomotive No. 7013 *Bristol Castle* (hastily renamed and renumbered as *Windsor Castle*) took over the role as royal engine to haul the funeral train from Paddington to Windsor on 15 February 1952. The engines never reverted to their original names and 7013 (aka 4082) was withdrawn from service in September 1964. Engine 4082 (aka 7013) was withdrawn in February 1965.

In more recent times, two Class 47 diesels, 47834 *Firefly* and 47835 *Windsor Castle* were nominated to haul royal trains. They were later renumbered and renamed 47798 *Prince William* and 47799 *Prince Henry* but were replaced in 2003 by two EWS Class 67 freight locomotives, 67005 *Queen's Messenger* and 67006 *Royal Sovereign*.

The cost of maintaining and using the royal train was £900,000 in 2011, paid out of the grant-in-aid that is voted by parliament to the royal household each year.

THE DOCKERS' UMBRELLA
The story of the Liverpool Overhead Railway

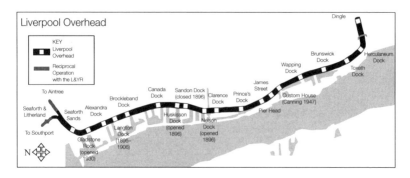

Liverpool's rapid growth as a major port during the 19th century soon led to serious congestion on the approach roads to the docks. The main artery linking all of these, Dock Road, became clogged with horse-drawn vehicles transporting goods to and from the ships, and the numerous railway level crossings only added to the delays. Not only were goods delayed but so too were the public.

To alleviate this congestion, a plan was put forward as early as 1852 to build an elevated passenger-carrying railway along the dock front. However, nothing came of this or a similar proposal put forward in 1877. Finally, in 1888, a group of local businessmen formed the Liverpool Overhead Railway Company and received permission from the Mersey Docks & Harbour Board to construct the much-needed new railway.

Work started in 1889 and a decision was made that the railway should be powered by electric traction which, at that time, was still in its infancy – thus making the Liverpool Overhead the world's first electric elevated city railway. It was also the first railway in the world to have an automatic electric signalling system. The standard gauge six-mile line, running from Seaforth Carriage Sheds in the north to Herculaneum Dock in the south, was officially

Liverpool Overhead

KEY

Liverpool Overhead

Reciprocal Operation with the L&YR

To Aintree

Seaforth & Litherland

To Southport

Seaforth Sands

Seaforth Dock

Alexandra Dock

Brockleband Dock

Gladstone Dock (opened 1930)

Langton Dock (1896–1906)

Canada Dock

Sandon Dock (closed 1896)

Huskisson Dock (opened 1896)

Clarence Dock

Nelson Dock (opened 1896)

Prince's Dock

James Street

Pier Head

Custom House (Canning 1947)

Wapping Dock

Brunswick Dock

Toxteth Dock

Herculaneum Dock

Dingle

N

opened on 4 February 1893 by the Marquis of Salisbury. There were 11 intermediate stations: Brocklebank Dock, Canada Dock, Sandon Dock, Clarence Dock, Princes Dock, Pier Head, James Street, Custom House, Wapping Dock, Brunswick Dock and Toxteth Dock. Initially, services began and ended at Alexandra Dock station in the north. Other

The Liverpool Overhead Railway in 1910

stations at Seaforth Sands, Langdon Dock, Huskisson Dock, Nelson Dock and a new southern terminus (underground!) at Dingle were opened in 1896.

> Although the railway suffered severe damage from German bombing raids during World War II, repairs were carried out quickly because of its strategic importance in the running of the overstretched docks.

The Liverpool Overhead Railway soon became affectionately known by its customers and local people as the 'Dockers' Umbrella'. There were no major accidents on the line and, up to the 1950s, it safely carried millions of dock workers along its route.

Escaping nationalisation in 1948, the railway company embarked on a modernisation programme for its ancient rolling stock; but despite this, the writing was soon on the wall for this unique British institution. In 1955, coupled with dwindling dock operations, it was found that the original iron viaducts that supported the line were badly corroded and required replacement. The cost of carrying out this work, estimated to be in the region of £2 million, was far beyond the financial means of the company and the line closed for good on 30 December 1956. Despite public protest and rescue attempts, the line had been completely dismantled by early 1959. Today, very little remains of this valuable part of Liverpool's heritage apart from the tunnel mouth to the old underground Dingle terminus.

THE STREAKERS
The story of Britain's streamlined steam locomotives

During the 1930s, with increased competition from road and rail travel, railways in the USA and Europe were competing with each other for the title of the 'World's Fastest Train'. Between 1932 and 1935 the Great Western Railway was the undisputed champion with the 'Cheltenham Flyer' for its non-stop journey between Swindon and Paddington. However, the introduction of the high-speed streamlined 'Flying Hamburger' articulated diesel train in Germany and the US 'Burlington Zephyr' changed all this. Suddenly, streamlining was in vogue, and in Britain, both the LMS and the LNER developed powerful streamlined 4-6-2 'Pacific' locomotives, built for speed.

LNER streamlined locomotives

In Britain, the first streamlined locomotive to be built was the 'W1' Class 4-6-4 high-pressure compound locomotive No. 10000. Designed by Nigel Gresley for the LNER, the loco was introduced in 1929 but was never a great success and was rebuilt as a three-cylinder engine in 1937.

Hauling a streamlined rake of seven articulated coaches, the first Class 'A4' loco in service, No. 2509 *Silver Link* reached a speed of 112.5mph on a test run in September 1935.

The first major class of streamlined locomotives to be built in Britain were the Gresley Class 'A4' Pacifics. Their famous wedge-shaped design was inspired by a French Bugatti diesel railcar that Gresley had seen on a trip to France. After intensive testing of models in a wind tunnel, the design was refined into the graceful locomotives that were introduced in 1935. First going into regular service on the new 'Silver Jubilee' express from King's Cross to Newcastle, these locomotives and their trains provided the LNER with an enormous public relations coup. High speed services to Edinburgh and Leeds were soon introduced, and the crowning glory came on 3 July 1938 when another locomotive of the 'A4' class, No. 4468 *Mallard*, achieved a world record

speed for a steam locomotive of 126mph on a test run down Stoke Bank. Although the streamlined side skirts were removed in later years to assist maintenance, the entire class of 34 locomotives retained their streamlined casing until finally withdrawn in the 1960s.

Buoyed by the success of the 'A4's, Gresley also added a similar streamlined casing to his Class 'P2' 2-8-2 locos in 1936. The first of these locos to be streamlined was No. 2001 *Cock o' the North,* but by 1944 all members of this class had been rebuilt as unstreamlined Class 'A2/2' 4-6-2s.

Gresley's final experiment in streamlining came in 1937 when he added streamlined casings similar to the 'A4' class to two members of the Class 'B17 Sandringham' 4-6-0 locomotives. The two locomotives treated were No. 2859 *East Anglian* and No. 2870 *City of London,* which were used to haul expresses between London Liverpool Street and Norwich from September 1937. The streamlining was removed from these two locos in 1951.

LMS streamlined locomotives

Not to be outdone by the LNER's success with streamlined trains, the LMS introduced its streamlined 'Princess Coronation' Class 4-6-2s in 1937. Designed by William Stanier to haul the crack 'Coronation Scot' express from London Euston to Glasgow, the first ten members of this class were fitted

On a test run on 27 June 1937, locomotive No. 6220 *Coronation* broke the then British speed record for steam locomotives when it achieved a speed of 114mph just south of Crewe – narrowly avoiding becoming derailed as it approached Crewe station at too high a speed!

with streamlined casings that had a rounded front end complete with 'speed whiskers' that extended along the side of the loco and tender and continued along the sides of the matching carriages. Two years later No. 6229 *Duchess of Hamilton* (renumbered and renamed as No. 6220 *Coronation*) visited the USA where it represented British railway achievement at the New York World's Fair. To reduce maintenance costs, the streamlined casing was removed from members of this class between 1946 and 1949.

GWR streamlined locomotives

Faced with the LNER's success, the GWR undertook a rather pathetic attempt to streamline two of its locomotives. 'Castle' Class 4-6-0 No. 5005 *Manorbier Castle* and 'King' Class 4-6-0 No. 6014 *King Henry VII* appeared in service in 1935, fitted with a round, bullet-shaped nose over the firebox door, streamlined casing over the outside cylinders and a continuous straight arch over the driving wheels. They also had a

The streamlined GWR 'King' Class 4-6-0 No. 6014 King Henry VII

V-shape to the front of the cab, a continuous roof linking the cab and tender and 'go-faster' fins behind the chimney and safety valves. The appearance of these once-graceful locomotives thus adorned was not the GWR's finest hour, and after a few years, the casings were removed and the experiment quietly forgotten!

Southern Railway air-smoothed locomotives

Last on the scene was the Southern Railway with the introduction of O.V. Bulleid's innovative air-smoothed 'Merchant Navy' Class 4-6-2 locomotives in 1941. Though not fully streamlined, these certainly gave the impression of speed. A total of 30 locomotives of this class were built between 1941 and 1949 but many of Bulleid's innovations proved costly to maintain and the locos were all rebuilt, minus casings, between 1956 and 1960.

KING'S CROSS STATION
G.K. Chesterton

This circled cosmos whereof man is god
   Has suns and stars of green and gold and red,
And cloudlands of great smoke, that range o'er range
   Far floating, hide its iron heavens o'erhead.

God! shall we ever honour what we are,
   And see one moment ere the age expire,
The vision of man shouting and erect,
   Whirled by the shrieking steeds of flood and fire?

Or must Fate act the same grey farce again,
   And wait, till one, amid Time's wrecks and scars,
Speaks to a ruin here, 'What poet-race
   Shot such cyclopean arches at the stars?'

MR BRADSHAW
– FRIEND OF THE RAILWAY TRAVELLER
The story of the railway timetable

George Bradshaw was born in Pendleton, Lancashire on 29 July 1801. He became an engraver and printer of canal maps in Manchester and, in 1838, published the world's first railway timetable. New railways were being opened at an ever-increasing rate, and to keep pace with this change, Bradshaw started issuing a revised edition once a month. Published in partnership with his London agent, William Jones Adams, and known as *Bradshaw's Monthly Railway Guide,* it was sold with a yellow cover and continued to be published until the final 1,521st edition in 1961.

From 1847 Bradshaw also published a *Continental Railway Guide,* and all railway timetables, irrespective of who published them, became known as 'Bradshaw's'.

In addition to introducing the world's first railway timetables, George Bradshaw also published the *Railway Manual* and the *Railway Shareholders' Guide*, both of which continued in print until 1922. In his private life, Bradshaw became a Quaker and peace activist and spent much of his time and money in helping the poor in his home city of Manchester. He died at 52 after contracting cholera in Norway in August 1853, and is buried in the grounds of Oslo cathedral. A portrait of Bradshaw, painted in 1841 by Richard Evans, hangs in the National Portrait Gallery in London.

The rapid growth of railways in Britain had a similar effect on the size of his timetable – in 1845 it consisted of only 32 pages but by 1898 it was nearly 1,000 pages!

Despite the success of Bradshaw's timetable, most railway companies started issuing their own timetables in the 1930s. On nationalisation of the railways in 1948, individual regional timetables were introduced by British Railways and it was only in 1974 that these were combined into an all-line timetable similar to

Bradshaw's original concept. Sadly, the final edition of the all-line UK railway timetable was published by Network Rail in May 2007. Costing £12 a copy, this bulky 2,500-page tome was latterly selling only about 20,000 copies per year. Apparently travellers now prefer to use the on-line timetables available at the touch of a button on their computer (assuming they have one).

Lynton to Red Wharf Bay via the scenic route

Prior to the antics of Ernest Marples MP and Dr Beeching (see pages 52–53), it was possible to travel from more or less anywhere to more-or-less anywhere else by train. Just for fun, let's look at a real journey that could be accomplished using *Bradshaw's July 1922 Railway Guide*. After a week's restful holiday at the Valley of Rocks Hotel in Lynton, North Devon, an intrepid traveller, for some reason forgotten in the mists of time, needs to journey to Red Wharf Bay in Anglesey during the week. It may be quicker by road in the 21st century but nowhere near as fun. This is how he fared:

DAY 1

Lynton & Lynmouth.....................*dep* 8.15am
Barnstaple Town............................ arr 9.37am

CHANGE

Barnstaple Town........................*dep* 10.12am
Bristol TM...................................... arr 1.34pm

CHANGE

Bristol TM................................. dep 2.00pm
Gloucester Eastgate .... arr 2.57pm

CHANGE

Gloucester Central...................... dep 3.47pm
Hereford .... arr 5.02pm

CHANGE

Hereford .... dep 8.45pm
Three Cocks
   Junction .... arr 9.49pm

CHANGE and stay the night in a local hostelry

DAY 2
Three Cocks
   Junction.................................*dep* 7.47am
Moat Lane Junction .... arr 9.40am

CHANGE

Moat Lane Junction.....................*dep* 9.55am
Machynlleth .... arr 10.43am

CHANGE

Machynlleth ....*dep* 10.45am
Afonwen.. arr 1.35pm

CHANGE

Afonwen..................................... dep 1.55pm
Bangor .... arr 3.10pm

CHANGE

Bangor .... dep 3.35pm
Gaerwen.. arr 3.55pm

CHANGE

Gaerwen...................................... dep 3.56pm
Holland Arms................................ arr 4.00pm

CHANGE

Holland Arms .... dep 4.33pm
Red Wharf Bay .... arr 4.54pm

Journey's end!

A QUICK SNOG IN THE BACK ROW
Some classic British railway films

The Wrecker (1929)

Based on a play written by Arnold Ridley, this silent black and white film included a spectacular crash sequence filmed on the Basingstoke & Alton Light Railway. Filmed by 22 cameras, the head-on crash was staged on a Sunday near the village of Herriard when no other trains were running. The line was cleared for normal running the next day. The 59-minute film was produced by Michael Balcon for Gainsborough Films, directed by Hungarian-born Geza von Bolvary and starred Carlyle Blackwell, Benita Hume and Joseph Striker. Some of the footage from this film was used in the 1936 film *Seven Sinners*.

Oh! Mr Porter (1937)

Filmed on the closed Basingstoke & Alton Light Railway just before the track was lifted, *Oh! Mr Porter* is set in Ireland and tells the hilarious story of Will Hay who is given the job as station master at the remote Buggleskelly station in Northern Ireland and uncovers a gang of gun-runners. Directed by Marcel Varnel, the 85-minute black and white film stars Will Hay, Moore Marriott and Graham Moffatt, The station scenes were shot at Cliddesden station just before it was demolished and the locomotive featured in the film was the Kent & East Sussex Railway's 2-4-0 tank *Northiam* (renamed *Gladstone* for the film) built by Hawthorn Leslie in 1899.

Brief Encounter (1945)

Based on a short play called *Still Life* by Noel Coward, *Brief Encounter* is a beautifully crafted love story of a man and a woman who meet briefly in a railway station refreshment room during World War II. Many sequences of the film were shot at Carnforth Station, renamed Milford Junction Station for the film, during the bitterly cold February of 1945. Filming of the platform scenes was carried out during the night after the last train had departed and continued through until the early morning. A mock-up of the exterior of the refreshment room was built at Carnforth while the interior shots were filmed at Denham Studios. The 85-minute black and white film was directed by David Lean and starred Celia Johnson, Trevor Howard and Stanley Holloway. Carnforth Station has recently been restored.

Capturing the atmosphere of a busy railway junction station during wartime, *Brief Encounter* includes some good shots of LMS Stanier Class '4' 2-6-4T No. 2429 hauling the local passenger train.

The Titfield Thunderbolt (1952)

This classic British comedy tells the story of a local community which reopens its branch line after it has been closed by British Railways. The railway scenes were shot on the picturesque Limpley Stoke to Camerton branch near Bath and at Temple Meads station in Bristol. The star of the film is undoubtedly the former Liverpool & Manchester Railway locomotive *Lion*, built in 1838, which ran under her own steam as the *Thunderbolt* and saved the day when the reopening of the line was sabotaged by a local bus company. Directed by Charles Crichton for Ealing Studios, the 84-minute colour film stars Stanley Holloway, Naunton Wayne, George Relph and John Gregson.

The Railway Children (1970)

The first major film to be shot entirely on a preserved railway, *The Railway Children* tells the story of a family who move from London to the country when their father is falsely sent to prison. It was shot on the Keighley & Worth Valley Railway in West Yorkshire and features several of that line's historic locomotives and rolling stock. Directed by Lionel Jeffries for EMI, Jenny Agutter, Bernard Cribbins and Dinah Sheridan star in the 102-minute colour film.

WHAT A WIND-UP!
The story of Frank Hornby and his tinplate trains

Frank Hornby was born in Liverpool on 15 May 1863. After leaving school he went to work in his father's provisions business as a junior cashier. When his father died, in 1887, Hornby joined a Liverpool meat importing business as a bookkeeper. In the same year he married Clara Godefroy and the couple produced two sons and a daughter.

While working as a bookkeeper, and with no experience in engineering, Hornby started to make toys out of sheet metal for his sons. He then hit upon the idea of cutting strips of perforated metal that could be joined together with nuts and bolts and in 1901 patented his idea as 'Improvements in Toy or Educational devices for Children and Young People'. Later marketed as 'Mechanics Made Easy' it became a worldwide hit. So Meccano was born.

Frank Hornby diversified his Meccano products and, in 1909, introduced the 'Hornby System of Mechanical Demonstration' in which Meccano was teamed up with pulleys and wheels to show the principles of mechanics.

By the outbreak of World War I in 1914, Meccano had become so successful that it was also being made in France and Germany, and at a new, purpose-built factory in Binns Road, Liverpool. The 'Hornby System of Mechanical Demonstration' range was further developed, and in 1915, Hornby introduced his first clockwork model railway game marketed under the name of Raylo.

After the war, during which the Binn's Road factory was turned over to producing munitions, Hornby went on to develop his first Gauge '0' toy train sets. First introduced in 1920, the clockwork trains were available in three colours to represent the London & North Western Railway, Midland Railway and Great Northern Railway systems. Each boxed set, costing 27s 6d (£1.37½p), contained a clockwork engine, tender and one truck, a set of tin plate rails, including a circle and two straights. The engine was fitted with reversing gear, brakes and regulator. Train sets followed in the colours of many other British and French railways.

These early Hornby trains were so successful that, within a few years, the range had developed to include much more realistic models of 4-4-0 tender and 4-4-2 tank engines, bogie coaches, bogie goods wagons, signalling, lamps, bridges, tunnels, level crossings, stations and complicated track layouts.

With an eye on the important North American market, Hornby introduced his first '0' gauge electric trains in 1925, but they were soon withdrawn from the home market because of the dangerously high voltage (220-240v AC) required to run them. Later, electric trains were introduced to run on a safer current of 4v DC, uprated to 6v DC in 1929. This range was expanded so that most of the Hornby train sets could be purchased in clockwork or electric variants.

> Probably the most detailed and accurate model that Hornby produced in '0' gauge was the beautiful 'Princess Elizabeth' 4-6-2. If you have a mint, boxed example of one of these engines then it could be worth over £2,000!

Frank Hornby had become a self-made millionaire by the 1930s and in 1931 was elected as Conservative MP for Everton. However, ill health forced him to quit politics in 1935. He lived long enough to see the introduction of his die-cast Dinky Toys range in 1934, but died from heart failure and diabetes on 21 September 1936. The first of the famous Hornby Dublo tabletop model railway sets were introduced in 1938.

After World War II, the Hornby range of '0' gauge tinplate trains became less popular and the range of train sets dwindled to a rather sad 0-4-0 clockwork locomotive, with four-wheeled coaches, chasing its tail around a circular track! This was not what the model railway market wanted and the range was completely discontinued in 1964, the year that Tri-ang Railways bought Meccano Ltd. A rather ignominious end to such an English institution!

ISLAND RAILWAYS
The story of some famous and some lesser known island railways and tramways around the coastline of Britain

Alderney, Channel Islands

Opened in 1847 to carry stone from Mannez Quarry for the construction of forts and the Braye breakwater, the standard gauge Alderney Railway was operated for many years by the British Admiralty. In 1980, the two-mile line was leased from the Home Office by the Alderney Railway Society. The railway now operates on Sundays from May to September, and on Saturdays in July and August, with trains departing from Braye Road station for the scenic journey to Mannez Quarry. Passengers are conveyed in former London Underground cars pushed and pulled by a small diesel locomotive. Beyond Braye Road station it is still possible to follow the disused and rusting rails down to the harbour and along the top of the breakwater.

> During the winter of 1911/1912, a loaded train ran off the end of the breakwater, and after that incident, all locomotives travelling along it had to carry lifebelts!

Anglesey/Holy Island

Both Anglesey, the largest island off the Welsh coast, and Holy Island have been connected to the national railway system since the opening of the Chester & Holyhead Railway in 1850. To carry trains across the Menai Strait, a new wrought iron tubular bridge, Britannia Bridge, was built by the railway's engineer, Robert Stephenson. The bridge was extensively damaged by fire in 1970 but has since been rebuilt on two levels, the upper one carrying a road and the lower one the railway. Main line trains still connect Holyhead with North Wales, Chester, Crewe and London. Branch lines once ran from Gaerwen to Amlwch and Holland Arms to Red Wharf Bay. The Amlwch branch was opened by the Anglesey Central Railway in 1864 and closed to passengers in 1964. Freight traffic continued until 1993 and since then the line has been mothballed. However, it is hoped that the line might reopen to passengers in the future. The Red Wharf Bay branch was opened in 1909; closed to passengers in 1930 and to goods in 1950.

Brownsea Island

Located in Poole Harbour and now owned by the National Trust, Brownsea Island is probably best known as the site of Robert Baden-Powell's first Scout camp that was held there in 1907. However, in 1852, a certain Colonel William Waugh bought Brownsea and embarked upon a massive development of the island. Included in his ambitious scheme was a pottery that was built on the south-west coast and linked by a horse-drawn tramway to a pier at the west end of the island. Within five years, Waugh's ambitious business empire on Brownsea had collapsed and the pottery and tramway closed.

Today, it is still possible to follow the route of the tramway southwards along the coast from Pottery Pier to the edge of the Scout Camp.

Isle of Bute

A 4ft gauge horse-drawn, passenger-carrying tramway was opened on the Isle of Bute in 1882. The only passenger tramway on a Scottish island, it was regauged to 3ft 6in and electrified in 1902. The route originally ran along the promenade at Rothesay and ended at Port Bannatyne. The double-track line was extended across the island to Ettrick Bay in 1905, giving a total length of nearly five miles; it remained in use until complete closure in 1936.

Flat Holm

Due to its strategic position on the approaches to Bristol and Cardiff in the Bristol Channel, Flat Holm was taken over by the military during World War II. From 1941, over 300 soldiers were based on the island, manning a range of heavy and light anti-aircraft guns and a radar station in the defence of the Bristol Channel ports. A light railway was constructed to convey provisions and ammunition from the pier at the north of the island to the various gun batteries, magazines and searchlight sites scattered around the island. Materials for the railway came from German 60cm gauge lines that had been captured during World War I and stored between the wars at the Longmoor Military Railway depot in Hampshire. The lines were lifted at the end of World War II by German prisoners of war; apart from traces of the track alignment, nothing remains of the railway today.

Hayling Island

A branch line from Havant to Hayling was opened for goods trains as far as Langstone in 1865. The route to South Hayling was completed in 1867 and passenger services started in July of that year. There were two intermediate stations at Langstone and North Hayling. From 1872 the line was operated by the London Brighton and South Coast Railway, becoming part of the Southern Railway in 1923.

Due to the cost of replacing the old timber railway bridge across Langstone Harbour, the line closed on 2 November 1963. The trackbed now forms the route of the Hayling Billy Trail, and the old station buildings at Hayling are now a theatre. There is still one railway operating on Hayling: opened in 2003, the 2ft gauge East Hayling Light Railway runs for about a mile through the sand dunes between the funfair at Beachlands and Eastoke Corner.

Isle of Man

The 3ft gauge Isle of Man Railway was opened in stages between 1873 and 1879 and did much to help the development of the island. Radiating out from Douglas, the extensive lines to Peel, Ramsey and Port Erin were all closed in 1965.

A privately funded and partially successful attempt was made to reopen the railway in 1967, but

Isle of Man Railway 2-4-0T No. 5 Mona, 1967

by the following year, the lines to Peel and Ramsey had finally closed. Under private ownership and with support from railway enthusiasts, the line to Port Erin soldiered on. Nationalised since 1976, the 15½-mile steam-operated line from

Douglas to Port Erin still remains in operation and its future seems assured.

During the height of the Victorian tourist boom on the Isle of Man, a unique and, at that time, technologically advanced electric railway was built northwards from Douglas following the beautiful and rugged coastline to the port of Ramsey. The 18-mile line was opened in stages between 1893 and 1899, and with a 5-mile branch to the summit of the island's only mountain, Snaefell (2,036ft above sea level), the line became an instant success with visitors. Surprisingly the main line operates on a 3ft gauge while the Snaefell branch is 3ft 6in gauge!

This scenic railway with its unique American-style trams was saved from closure in 1957 when it was nationalised by the Manx government. With much of the rolling stock still in its original form, a trip on this historic line is like a trip back in time!

Isle of Sheppey

Located just off the Kent coast, the Isle of Sheppey has been linked by rail to the mainland since 1860 when the London Chatham & Dover Railway opened its line to the port of Sheerness. The railway crosses the stretch of water known as The Swale on the combined road and rail Kingsferry Bridge, which has an electrically operated lifting section to allow the passage of ships.

During the early 20th century, attempts were made to develop the eastern coast of the Isle of Sheppey as a seaside resort. A light railway was opened in 1901 from the main railway line at Queenborough to the new resort of Leysdown-on-Sea. But the attempts to popularise Leysdown as a resort for Londoners was never a complete success and the railway closed in 1950.

The only trains currently operating on the Isle of Sheppey run between Sheerness and Sittingbourne, where there are connections with main line services.

Isle of Wight

Once upon a time the Isle of Wight boasted 56 miles of standard gauge public railway! Today, apart from the 5-mile Isle of Wight Steam Railway, which operates a steam-hauled service between Smallbrook Junction and Wootton, and the electrified 8½-mile section from Ryde Pier Head to Shanklin with its former London Underground stock, all this has disappeared.

L&SWR Class '02' No. 14 Fishbourne *being serviced*

Between 1862 and 1900, a total of six routes were built and, until the grouping of 1923, these were operated by three separate companies. The Isle of Wight Central Railway operated the lines between Smallbrook Junction to Cowes via Newport, Newport to Sandown via Merstone, and Merstone to Ventnor West. The Freshwater, Yarmouth & Newport Railway operated the line between Freshwater and Newport, and the Isle of Wight Railway ran services between Ryde (St Johns Road) and Ventnor and the branch from Brading to Bembridge. A joint line was opened between Ryde (St John's Road) and Ryde Pier Head by the LSWR and LBSCR in 1880.

Closures began under British Railways in the 1950s and culminated in 1966 with the ending of steam haulage and closure of all remaining routes apart from the Ryde to Shanklin section.

Jersey, Channel Islands

Two separate railways were built on the Channel Island of Jersey during the 19th century. The Jersey Railway opened between St Helier and St Aubin in 1870. The railway was built to the British standard gauge but later converted to 3ft 6in gauge when it was extended to Corbière.

Plans to electrify the 7-mile-long line in 1906

> Today, the former terminus building at St Aubin is now a police station and the trackbed of the railway line between St Aubin and Corbière has been converted to a cycle way and footpath.

did not materialise, and the railway closed for good in 1936 following a serious fire at St Aubin station when most of the rolling stock was destroyed.

The second railway on Jersey, the Jersey Eastern Railway, ran from St Helier to Gorey and was opened in 1872. However, increasing competition from buses led to its closure in 1929.

The trackbeds of both these railways were incorporated into the military network of railway lines that were built to link stone quarries and construction sites on Jersey during the German Occupation of World War II.

Lindisfarne or Holy Island

Located just off the coast of Northumberland, the island of Lindisfarne is an unlikely place to find the remains of a railway. However, in 1860, a Scottish company greatly expanded the limestone quarrying industry on the island and constructed lime kilns, a horse-drawn tramway and a jetty adjacent to the historic Lindisfarne Castle.

Although this ambitious venture had closed by 1900, visitors to the island and its castle can still walk along the well-preserved remains of the old tramway trackbed with its embankments and stone bridges.

Lundy Island

Windswept Lundy Island, 7 miles north of Hartland Point in Devon, was purchased by William Hudson Heaven in 1834. In an attempt to bring employment to Lundy, Heaven opened granite quarries on the east side of the island in 1863 and built a horse-drawn tramway to convey stone from the quarries to a landing stage where it was loaded on to ships. The quarries did not prove to be commercially viable and were closed in 1868. Today, visitors to the island, which is owned by the National Trust and managed by the Landmark Trust, can still follow the clearly defined route of the old tramway.

Isle of Mull

Opened in 1984, Mull Rail was the only passenger-carrying railway to operate on a Scottish island. This 10¼in gauge miniature railway carried visitors for

1¼ miles from a station near Craignure Pier, served by Caledonian MacBrayne ferries from Oban, to Torosay Castle. Building this little railway was no mean feat as it involved rock blasting and crossing a bog. Sadly this little railway closed in 2011.

Orkney Islands

A group of about 50 islands lying off the north coast of Scotland, the Orkneys have a fascinating railway history. Many standard gauge and narrow gauge lines were built between the end of the 19th century through to World War II to serve quarries, military installations and a lighthouse service depot.

By far the largest network of lines were those built by Balfour Beatty during the construction of the Churchill Barriers during World War II. These enormous concrete barriers, designed to protect the strategic naval anchorage at Scapa Flow, connected the Orkney mainland with South Ronaldsay across the islands of Burray, Glimsholm and Lambholm. Both 3ft gauge and standard gauge lines were used to convey the vast amount of building material required to construct the barriers.

> Today, discerning visitors to these islands can still find many traces of this once strategically important network of the most northerly of our railway lines.

Steep Holm

As with neighbouring Flat Holm, the little island of Steep Holm was taken over by the military during World War II to protect the approaches to Bristol and Cardiff. Starting in 1941, army engineers installed four 6in World War I naval guns, together with their emplacements, look-outs and ammunition stores, at strategic points around the edge of the island's plateau.

To transport the huge amounts of these building materials, the army built a jetty, linked to the plateau by a narrow gauge switchback railway, built from captured German World War I prefabricated 60cm gauge lines. This switchback route was cable-operated with diesel-powered winches hauling wagons up the three inclines from the jetty. Unlike Flat Holm, nearly all the track is still *in situ*, and visitors to the island can follow the railway's zig-zag route to the top.

THE SEND-OFF
By Wilfred Owen

Down the close, darkening lanes they sang their way
To the siding-shed,
And lined the train with faces grimly gay.

Their breasts were stuck all white with wreath and spray
As men's are, dead.
Dull porters watched them, and a casual tramp
Stood staring hard,
Sorry to miss them from the upland camp.
Then, unmoved, signals nodded, and a lamp
Winked to the guard.

So secretly, like wrongs hushed-up, they went.
They were not ours;
We never heard to which front these were sent.
Nor there if they yet mock what women meant
Who gave them flowers.

Shall they return to beatings of great bells
In wild train-loads?
A few, a few, too few for drums and yells,
May creep back, silent, to village wells
Up half-known roads.

A RAILWAY INSTITUTION
The story of the GWR Swindon Mechanics Institution

By 1905, Swindon, where the locomotive, carriage and wagon works of the Great Western Railway were situated, had grown in 60 years from a small village into a corporate town of 50,000 inhabitants, 13,000 of which were in the direct employ of the railway company. In that year, the wages bill for its Swindon staff cost the GWR £16,000 per week. The centre of the educational and social activities of the town was the GWR Swindon Mechanics Institution, which was 'instituted on the 8 January 1844, for the purpose of disseminating useful knowledge and encouraging rational amusement amongst all classes of people employed by the Great Western Railway.'

Subscription to the institute ranged from fourpence to tenpence (pre-decimal money!) a month for GWR men, while female employees of the company were provided with a special ladies-only reading room.

The institute in Swindon provided its members with circulating and reference libraries, reading rooms and rooms for billiards, chess, draughts and other games, a large hall for musical, dramatic and other entertainments, a lecture hall and classrooms for educational purposes. Persons not employed by the GWR could also join the institute but their subscription was markedly higher.

In addition to its everyday work, the institute arranged two great annual events. The first was a trip, which was held in July. For this the GWR provided free special excursion trains to many destinations. In 1904, 23,145 members took part, of which 9,744 were children. For this event, the GWR laid on 21 special trains, which left Swindon between 4am and 7am on that same July morning. There were three trains to Weston-super-Mare, five trains to Weymouth, three trains to London, one train to Winchester, one train to Birkenhead via Worcester and Chester, and another to Manchester via Birmingham and Crewe. There were also three trains to South Wales, and four trains all calling at Exeter, Newton Abbot and Plymouth. Some of the passengers returned the same day, others stayed away for a week, and all travelled free, provided they conformed to the regulations and used only the trains specified in the programme.

The second event was a children's fête, usually held in August in the town's park, which had been given to the town by the GWR. There was a large programme of attractions, musical bands and a firework display as well as free refreshments provided for the children. During the 1904 fête, three tons of cake was consumed, each portion of which weighed 5lb!

Along with the Swindon Mechanics Institution and light years before the NHS was ever created, membership of the GWR Medical Fund Society, established in 1847, was compulsory for all staff employees of the GWR in Swindon. With a staff of 11 doctors, a dental surgeon and his assistant and seven dispensing chemists, the society ran a well-appointed cottage hospital, a dentistry, a commodious dispensary, washing and Turkish baths, swimming baths, hairdressing and shaving saloons, and also provided wheelchairs for the benefit of its members. The subscriptions paid by employees also enabled them to use a number of other hospitals and convalescent homes in the Swindon area. The company certainly looked after its employees then!

Although working conditions and hours were much harsher and longer than those of today, the GWR's paternalistic attitude to staff, however lowly, engendered a fierce loyalty that was passed down through the generations. I doubt if employees of modern-day train operators can say the same.

ONCE THERE WERE ONLY FIELDS
The story of Crewe railway works

Unlike the GWR, which concentrated all of its major plant works in a single centre, the London & North Western Railway (later forming part of the LMS) had three railway towns: Crewe, in Cheshire, where the company's locomotive and steel works were situated; Wolverton, in Buckinghamshire, the site of the carriage works; and Earlstown, in Lancashire, site of the wagon works. The largest, by far, was at Crewe where the Grand Junction Railway established its works in 1843.

Before 1843, the whole area now occupied by the town and works of Crewe was agricultural land. Within three years of the Grand Junction Railway moving in, the population stood at a few hundred, yet by the early 20th century it had grown to 40,000 (today, the population is around 70,000). The men employed in the works originally numbered 161 but by 1904 it had grown to 8,000, not including large numbers of men employed in other departments of the railway company's service.

In 1855, in order to encourage students, the directors of the L&NWR gave a donation of £20 to be awarded in books as prizes for literary and scientific attainments to servants of the company under the age of 21 employed in the locomotive department.

The London & North Western Railway was formed in 1846 by its amalgamation with the London & Birmingham and Manchester & Birmingham Railways. Before this the Grand Junction had already provided its men in Crewe with a library and reading room, and given a donation to purchase books. In 1845, this movement developed into the Crewe Mechanics' Institution. In 1849, evening classes for teaching reading, writing, arithmetic and mechanical drawing were formed in connection with the institute. Nearly all of the teachers at the institute were also engaged at Crewe Works and so provided first-hand knowledge to their pupils. Scholarships were also endowed, to be awarded to young men employed at all of the L&NWR works and, from 1872, many students of the institution, all of whom were employed at Crewe works, won the coveted Whitworth national scholarship.

L&NWR 2-2-2 No. 117 Tiger, near Weedon, 1900

Importantly, membership of the Crewe Mechanics' Institution was always open to non-employee residents of the town for nominal fees.

In addition to providing educational needs, the L&NWR established a small hospital at Crewe in 1863. This was extended on several occasions and rebuilt in 1900 with accommodation for 16 in-patients. The hospital, entirely supported by the company, provided free medical facilities for all of its employees in the town. As well as the churches and schools it provided, the company also built 800 homes in Crewe for its key employees, and donated a park to the town. To keep pace with modern technology, the L&NWR also opened an electrical engineering laboratory at Crewe in the early 20th century.

After the 'Big Four' Grouping in 1923 (see pages 70–71), Crewe Works, with its own steel-producing plant, manufactured more powerful and modern steam locomotives for the newly formed LMS. At its peak, Crewe Works employed over 20,000 people and under its new Chief Mechanical Engineer, William Stanier (see pages 38–39), it turned out the superb 'Princess' and 'Coronation' Class 4-6-2s along with the versatile 'Black Fives' and 'Jubilees'.

By 1990, over 8,000 locomotives had been built at Crewe since its opening in 1843. Sadly, what is left of Crewe Works is a shadow of its former self and much of the site is now occupied by supermarkets, a leisure park and a health centre.

WORKING FOR 'THE FIRM'
Employment prospects during the golden age of railways

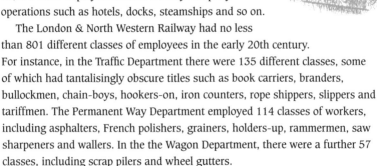

By the dawn of the 20th century the railways were one of the main employers in Britain. Of the 600,000 or so people employed by the railways, more than half constituted the managerial and operating staff of the lines. About 200,000, or one-third of the total, were engaged in the maintenance and renewal of the permanent way and rolling stock, while the remaining 80,000 were employed in other railway company operations such as hotels, docks, steamships and so on.

The London & North Western Railway had no less than 801 different classes of employees in the early 20th century. For instance, in the Traffic Department there were 135 different classes, some of which had tantalisingly obscure titles such as book carriers, branders, bullockmen, chain-boys, hookers-on, iron counters, rope shippers, slippers and tariffmen. The Permanent Way Department employed 114 classes of workers, including asphalters, French polishers, grainers, holders-up, rammermen, saw sharpeners and wallers. In the the Wagon Department, there were a further 57 classes, including scrap pilers and wheel gutters.

The average amount paid weekly by the L&NWR in wages was about £87,000 in 1904. The salaried staff of the company were paid monthly or, in some cases, fortnightly.

Altogether, the mighty London & North Western Railway employed a total of 82,835 people in 1904, of which only 1,542 were women. Although not taking into account the very many subdivisions, some of which are listed above, the general classification and subdivision of labour was as follows:

Personnel of the L&NWR in 1904

Principal officers 110
Brakesmen 2,139
Capstan men 358
Capstan lads 17
Carmen (adult) 3,657
Carmen (junior) 1,315
Carriage cleaners (adult) 1,050
Carriage cleaners (junior) 54
Carriage and wagon examiners 368
Checkers (adult) 1,875
Checkers (junior) 45
Checkers, chain-boys and slippers
    (adult) 20
Checkers, chain-boys and slippers
    (junior) 51
Clerks (adult) 7,320
Clerks (junior) 1,953
Engine cleaners (adult) 2,448
Engine cleaners (junior) 533
Engine drivers 4,085
Firemen 2,868
Gatekeepers 249
Greasers (adult) 97
Greasers (junior) 30
Guards (passenger) 629
Horsedrivers (shunting) 180
Inspectors (permanent way) 68
Inspectors (others) 554
Labourers (adult) 9,290
Labourers (junior) 548
Lampmen 201

Lamp-lads 8
Loaders and sheeters 673
Mechanics (adult) 10,948
Mechanics (junior) 2,138
Messengers (adult) 110
Messengers (junior) 495
Number takers (adult) 42
Number takers (junior) 95
Permanent way men 7,276
Pointsmen (ground) 18
Policemen 103
Porters (adult) 6,151
Porters (junior) 1,135
Shunters 1,348
Signal fitters /telegraph wiresmen 115
Signalmen 3,025
Signalbox lads 67
Station masters and goods agents 877
Ticket collectors and examiners 265
Watchmen 72
Yardsmen 102
Foremen (permanent way) 14
Bus drivers 24
Point cleaners 58
Stablemen and horsekeepers 327
Miscellaneous (adults) 3,067
Miscellaneous (junior) 395

TOTAL 82,835

WHAT A BORE!
The story of the Severn Tunnel

A map from 1946 showing the route of the tunnel and the surrounding area

Even before the railways were built, the River Severn was an obstacle to traffic between southwest England and South Wales. Rudimentary ferries had existed since Roman times, but until the opening of the Severn Railway Bridge in 1879 and the Severn Tunnel in 1886, the lowest physical crossing was higher up the river at Gloucester. The coming of the railways to the region in the 1840s changed all this and it soon became apparent that a lower crossing was essential to avoid the circuitous route through Gloucester.

As a temporary measure, a rail-connected steam passenger ferry came into operation on the New Passage route in 1863. In the same year, the engineer in charge of the building of the ferry jetties, Charles Richardson, unsuccessfully put a Bill before Parliament seeking powers to build a railway tunnel under the river. Over the next few years ferry traffic became so heavy that the building of a tunnel became a priority.

Finally, in 1872, the Great Western Railway obtained the authority to build the tunnel when the Severn Tunnel Railway Act was passed by Parliament.

Excluding its approaches, the length of the tunnel is 4 miles 624 yards and, excepting the London Underground system, until the opening of Phase 2 of the Channel Tunnel Link, was the longest main line railway tunnel in the UK.

Richardson was appointed engineer and Sir John Hawkshaw the consulting engineer. The route of the tunnel and its approaches, runs from Pilning in Gloucestershire to Rogiet (later called Severn Tunnel Junction) in Monmouthshire.

Construction began in 1873 but progress was slow and by 1877 less than a mile had been excavated under the river. To speed up construction, the GWR let two contracts for sinking new shafts and headings, one from the Gloucestershire side and the other from the Monmouthshire side. On the latter side an iron-lined shaft was also sunk at Sudbrook to accommodate the massive steam-driven pumping engines that were required to keep the tunnel from flooding.

By October 1879, the two headings were only 130 yards apart when a major setback happened. During excavations, a previously unknown enormous fresh-water spring, later known as the Great Spring, suddenly broke into the heading on the Monmouthshire side at the rate of 6,000 gallons a minute and totally overwhelmed the pumping engines. Work recommenced a year later after divers with the latest self-contained breathing apparatus managed to isolate the Great Spring. The two headings finally met under the river on 26 September 1881.

Over the next four years work was further delayed on several occasions when the tunnel was again flooded, not only by the Great Spring, but also by a tidal wave that swept up the Severn estuary in 1883.

The brickwork lining of the tunnel was completed in April 1885 and by September the double-tracked permanent way had also been laid. Sir Daniel Gooch, Chairman of the GWR, travelled through the tunnel in a special train on 5 September. Opening for normal traffic was delayed soon afterwards when sections of the brick lining started to disintegrate under pressure from the water in the surrounding rock. With more powerful pumps and a ventilation system installed at Sudbrook, the Severn Tunnel, then the longest underwater tunnel in the world, was officially opened to goods traffic on 1 September 1886 and to passengers at the beginning of December.

The railway tunnel is still open to traffic and the Sudbrook pumping engines, converted to run on electricity in the early 1960s, pump an estimated 30 million gallons a day to prevent flooding.

FROM GUNBOATS TO CORPSES
The story of unusual railway traffic

A century ago it was possible, given the appropriate notice, to send virtually anything by train, and the railway companies went out of their way to try to accommodate their customers, no matter how unusual the request.

The L&NWR showed just how accommodating it could be when asked to carry a gunboat from London to Liverpool in 1904. The boat's dimensions, 75ft 3in long, 6ft 3in deep and 9ft 8in wide, exceeded the L&NWR's loading gauge, but with only a few days notice, the company managed to get the gunboat to Liverpool in time for it to be loaded on to a departing liner.

The work was carried out on Sunday, 31 July – which being before August Bank Holiday, was not very convenient. The gunboat was mounted on a trolley 3ft 8in above rail level, so as to clear the sides of the station platforms. During the whole of its journey over the 194 miles between London and Liverpool, the section of line adjoining the track on which it was running was kept closed, so as to prevent collision with any passing train. In short, single-line working was put into force, section by section, over the whole of the company's main line to Liverpool.

> For the conveyance of very heavy loads, special types of wagons were employed, one of which was known as a platform wagon, the platform being suspended between two four-wheeled bogie trucks.

Some of the consignments that railway companies had to carry were extremely curious. One such item was a 12ft high stone figure in human form that was an undelivered consignment and remained in one of the company's warehouses in London for over 30 years. The figure, believed to be the fossilised remains of an Irish giant, was excavated near the Giants' Causeway in Northern Ireland; after appearing in various exhibitions, it was conveyed from Manchester to London on 28 August 1876. However, the original consignee had died and the L&NWR was prevented by law from selling it. By 1904 the warehouse rent for the figure had accumulated to £175. Permission was eventually given for its sale, which took place at the L&NWR's annual salvage auction.

40 tons of silkworms' eggs were once sent by the L&NWR for shipment to Japan, and great care had to be taken to keep them cool in case they hatched out on their journey.

A corpse was a very expensive consignment to send by rail 100 years ago, the uniform charge being one shilling per mile. However, several cases occurred in which an attempt was made to evade this expense by concealing the nature of the consignment.

One of the strangest cases was a large box that had arrived at a London goods station without an invoice giving particulars of its destination. It being customary for railway staff to trace the missing information, the box was opened to reveal what appeared to be a dead body. The police were called and they decided that the body should be sent to the nearest mortuary, where in due course it was 'sat upon' by a coroner, assisted by 12 'good men and true'. They concluded that the contents of the box was undoubtedly a corpse, but that it had been dead for some years and that its discovery did not point to any recent crime. The body was then buried, but subsequently the invoice turned up, revealing that the box had contained a mummy and that its destination was a museum in Belgium. The remains eventually reached the museum but in a rather damaged condition.

Some time afterwards, the railway company received a very indignant letter from a lady in Peru who complained that, due to the negligence of the railway authorities, the mummified remains of a Peruvian Inca which she had sent to Belgium arrived at its destination in a condition not fit for exhibition. Although the railway company denied negligence, the Courts decided against it and it was forced to pay heavy damages to the aggrieved consignee of the mummy!

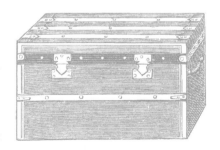

GEE UP!
The story of the railway horse

Until well into the 20th century, the horse played an important role in the running of Britain's railways. In the very early days of the railways, horses were often employed to haul trains until they were superseded by steam traction. However, thousands of horses were employed by the railway companies for shunting in goods yards and for delivery of goods by road until nationalisation in 1948.

Shunting horses were mainly employed at small country stations for the movement of single wagonloads, and were much more cost-effective and efficient than using a steam locomotive. However, these horses were prone to injury through catching their feet on or between rails or tripping over the numerous bars and wires that abounded at busy junctions. They were gradually replaced by hydraulic or electric capstans but the last two, at Newmarket station, were not retired until as late as 1967.

> Two horse-drawn services lingered on into the 20th century: the Port Carlisle branch until 1914, when horses were replaced by steam; and the Inchture branch in Scotland until 1917, when the line closed.

The use of horses for delivery of goods by road was widespread and in the early days this service was supplied by independent carriers who had been in business long before the advent of the railways. These old firms, such as Pickford and Chaplin & Horne, did not give up their former priority without a struggle. Partnership arrangements were made between the new railway companies and the carriers, and for many years railway companies, such as the GWR, did not own a single horse and cart. But as the railways pushed their way into new districts which had no carriers, or where, on entering a town, they found the existing cartage connections had already been sewn up by their rival, it became necessary for the companies to organise their own collection and delivery service.

By the beginning of the 20th century the majority of goods being carried to and from railway stations, yards and warehouses was almost exclusively in the hands of the railway companies' own teams. So rather than writing off the horse as a means of transport, the coming of the railways had brought about an enormous increase in the use of this animal.

To stable hundreds of horses in large cities such as London, Glasgow, Liverpool, Birmingham or Leeds was difficult without massive expenditure for land, as the majority of animals needed to be housed within a short distance of the central goods depots. Companies often converted arches under their

In 1904, London & North Western Railway and Midland Railway each owned over 5,000 horses; Great Northern Railway had 2,782; Great Western 2,668; Lancashire & Yorkshire 1,867; and Great Eastern 1,745.

viaducts into stables, while underground stables were also built beneath railway buildings. The more modern stables built at the beginning of the 20th century, however, were constructed on upper floors of premises devoted to other uses. In 1904, the GWR stables near Paddington housed 626 horses in a four-storey building, while the Great Northern Railway accommodated 189 horses in three storeys above a goods warehouse in Clerkenwell. In addition to stables, other buildings were erected by the railway companies as provender stores, shoeing forges, harness factories and horse hospitals. One store was built by the Great Eastern Railway near Romford to produce the feed mixture for its 1,745 horses.

After World War I, railway horses were gradually replaced by motor lorries to deliver goods by road. Even so, at the time of nationalisation in 1948, the newly formed British Transport Commission had over 9,000 of these magnificent creatures on its payroll!

ALONG STRANGE LINES
Some little known and unusual railways

Listowel & Ballybunion Railway

One of the most unusual railways ever built, the Listowel & Ballybunion Railway, was opened on 1 March 1888: it connected the market town of Listowel with the small seaside resort of Ballybunion on Ireland's west coast. This 9-mile long monorail, the first of its kind in the world, was built on the Lartigue principle, which had been invented by French engineer Charles Lartigue (1834–1907) after he saw how camels carried heavy loads across the Algerian desert.

Lartigue's monorail system consisted of a single rail track that was carried about 3ft above ground on A-shaped trestles. Wagons were designed to run on a system of grooved wheels grouped in sets of bogies along the track with their balanced loads carried on each side like the panniers on a camel.

> Lartigue espoused the monorail's advantages over normal railway lines, including its ability to negotiate sharp curves and its much cheaper construction and running costs.

Lartigue's first operating monorail system, a 60-mile line built in 1881 to carry esparto grass across the Algerian desert, did not involve steam locomotives but depended on mules to pull the trains of loaded panniers. By 1886 Lartigue had developed a steam locomotive that could operate on his system and exhibited a full-scale working layout in Tothill Fields, Victoria Street, Westminster, London to show how a monorail could be used for military, agricultural, industrial or passenger purposes.

Meanwhile, public pressure was on in the Irish county of Kerry to build a railway to link the market town of Listowel with the small seaside resort of Ballybunion. Various proposals had been put forward but had come to nothing until a bill was put forward for Parliamentary approval to construct the line using the Lartigue monorail system. The bill was given royal assent on

16 April 1886 and the Listowel & Ballybunion Railway Company was born. By the following year, an order had been placed with the Hunslet Engine Company of Leeds for three unique 0-3-0 steam locomotives, and construction of the line was proceeding rapidly. The first public trains ran on 5 March 1888 and, for a while, this unique railway brought much national and international fame to this rural part of Ireland.

A locomotive and passenger car of the Lartigue Monorail

Sadly, although much used and loved by local people, over the next 34 years the little railway was never really financially viable. The end came following several years of vandalism and sabotage inflicted on it during the Irish Civil War, and the last train ran on 14 October 1924. However, the story has a happy ending as a short section of monorail track, with trains hauled by a replica steam-outline 0-3-0 diesel, began operating near the site of the original Lartigue terminus in Listowel in 2003.

Potato railways of Lincolnshire

Few people know of this once-extensive network of narrow gauge lines that were built haphazardly from the early 20th century to serve the potato fields and farms of Lincolnshire. At its height in the late 1920s, the disjointed and unconnected network, mainly located in the south east of the county around Spalding, had a total mileage of over 100 miles serving over 30 separate farms.

By far the largest of the railway networks was the Nocton Estate Railway, which at its peak extended to over 20 miles of track. This network served all parts of the large estate including running through the piggery, sheep pens and potato-chitting house. Although steam locos were unsuccessfully used for a short period, motive power was usually supplied by diminutive petrol-engined

Many of the lightly laid lines were built using Army surplus track to a 60cm gauge and employed either horse or locomotive power to haul their loaded wagons of potatoes to the nearest standard gauge railhead.

Simplex locomotives. The estate was purchased by Smith's, the makers of the original potato crisps, in 1938 and most of the railway continued in use until 1960 when new farm roads were built and lorries introduced. Other extensive networks in Lincolnshire included the 13 miles of the Fleet Light Railway at Fleet and 10 miles at the Dennis Estates near Deeping St Nicholas.

Closures started in the late 1930s and accelerated after World War II until the last short length of line still in operation on the Nocton estate closed in 1969. Today, apart from a few preserved items of rolling stock at the Lincolnshire Coast Light Railway Historical Vehicles Trust at Winthorpe, near Skegness, nothing now remains of this little known gem of British railway history.

Lochaber Narrow Gauge Railway

Another little known railway, the Lochaber Narrow Gauge Railway, was originally built as a temporary line by the civil engineering contractors Balfour Beatty during the construction of a massive hydro-electric scheme to provide electricity for a new British Aluminium Company plant at Fort William. Work commenced in 1925 with the construction of a short 3ft gauge line from a pier on Loch Linnhe to the site of the proposed aluminium works, otherwise known during construction as 'Base Camp'. Once the works was operating, this stretch of line was also used for the import of raw alumina and the export of aluminium ingots.

A tunnel, 15 miles long and 15ft in diameter, had to be excavated between Loch Treig and Base Camp

Together with fairly steep gradients, construction of the line also involved the building of over 50 timber trestle bridges and branch lines, some built to 2ft gauge, that serviced the various tunnel adits.

to carry the enormous quantities of water that were required to power the generating turbines at the new power plant. As there was no road access to this remote part of Scotland, a further 19 miles of 3ft gauge railway, known as the Upper Works Railway, was built by the contractors from Base Camp up to Loch Treig to support this massive construction project, which also involved the building of two massive dams. Although intended to be a temporary measure, the Lochaber Narrow Gauge Railway actually remained in operation for over 40 years. Aluminium production began in 1929 and in 1935 it was decided to retain the railway to support the servicing and maintainance of this enormous project. Motive power over the years was provided by a mixture of steam, petrol, diesel and battery locomotives along with several passenger-carrying Wickham 'speeders'.

The end came as late as the 1970s. Firstly the Pier Railway was closed and, with new access roads being built, the future of the Upper Works Railway started to look uncertain. Following heavy rainfall and flooding in October 1971, part of the line was washed away, never to be replaced. The railway still continued to operate in a piecemeal fashion until the last section of Upper Works Railway finally disappeared in early 1977.

Volk's Electric Railway

The first electric railway in Britain and the oldest still operating in the world, Volk's Electric Railway was opened in 1883 for a quarter of a mile along Brighton's seafront between the Aquarium and Chain Pier. Designed by inventor and engineer, Magnus Volk, it was an instant hit with holidaymakers.

First built to a gauge of 2ft, it was regauged in 1884 to 2ft 8½in. In 1901, the line was extended to Black Rock, giving it a total length of a mile and a quarter. More cars were added and power began to be supplied from Brighton's mains electricity, converted to 160 volts DC. By the 1920s the little line was carrying over a million passengers a year.

The railway, a fitting memorial to Victorian inventiveness, currently operates services between Black Rock and the pier from Easter to the end of September.

CLIFFHANGERS
The story of Britain's funicular railways

Funicular, or cliff railways, have been an attraction at many resorts in England and Wales since late Victorian times. A large number of these unique cable-operated railways were built by the engineer George Marks with the financial backing of publishing tycoon, George Newnes. Originally, nearly all the lines were powered by a water-balance system, but most were later converted to electricity.

With gradients as steep as 1 in 1.15 and gauges that varied from 3ft to 7ft 6in, the majority were built at seaside resorts to convey holidaymakers up and down steep cliffs from the town to the beach. The first to be built was opened in Scarborough in 1875. The most recent, the Cairngorm Funicular Railway near Aviemore, was opened in 2001 to replace the existing chair lifts.

Many cliff railways have long since closed but some are still operating today and there are even plans for more to be built.

The Bridgnorth Cliff Railway

Lynton and Lynmouth Cliff Railway in 2003

Cliff Railways Operating in Britain

Aberystwyth
Constitution Hill Cliff
  Railway
Opened: 1896

Aviemore
Cairngorm Funicular
  Railway
Opened: 2001

Blaenau Ffestiniog
Llechwedd Slate Caverns
Opened: 1979

Bournemouth
East Cliff Lift
Opened: 1908

Bournemouth
Fisherman's Walk Lift
Opened: 1935

Bournemouth
West Cliff Lift
Opened: 1908

Bridgnorth
Castle Hill Railway
Opened: 1892

Folkestone
Leas Lift
Opened: 1885

Hastings
East Hill Lift
Opened: 1903

Hastings
West Hill Lift
Opened: 1891

Llwyngwern
Centre for Alternative
  Technology, nr
  Machynlleth
Opened: 1992

Lynton
Lynton & Lynmouth Cliff
  Railway
Opened: 1890

Saltburn-by-the-Sea
Saltburn Inclined
  Tramway
Opened: 1883

Scarborough
Central Tramway
Opened: 1881

Scarborough
South Cliff Tramway
Opened: 1875

Scarborough
St Nicholas Cliff Lift
Opened: 1929

Shipley Glen
Shipley Glen Tramway
Opened: 1895
Closed pending repair

Southend-on-Sea
Southend Cliff Railway
Opened: 1912

Torquay
Babbacombe Cliff
  Railway
Opened: 1926

Wakefield
National Coal Mining
  Museum
Opened: 1988

Windsor
Legoland
Opened: 1991

SMILE PLEASE!
Two famous British railway photographers

R. C. Riley (1921– 2006)

As a keen trainspotter in the late 1950s and 1960s I can recall often seeing the name 'R. C. Riley' as a photo credit in my *ABC* books, *Trains Illustrated* and *Railway Magazine*. Little did I then know that, years later, I would one day meet this revered gentleman through my work as a book designer. In the following years, until his death in 2006, I had on many occasions to seek his help in obtaining some rare and very specific railway image – if he couldn't supply it then he definitely knew someone who could! With his immense knowledge of the subject, Dick was always ready to help, and was always the perfect gentleman. He also had some great stories to tell about his early railway photography jaunts. Here are a few of them:

> In 1950 Dick was concerned with travelling over and photographing all surviving Western Region lines still open to passengers. This task was virtually completed in the summer of 1951, when, with the aid of a monthly return from Paddington to Aberystwyth (£3 3s 11d, or £3.20), he travelled out via Shrewsbury and back via Carmarthen. In 16 days he travelled over 1,944 miles at a cost of £9 13s 4½d (£9.68). Those were the days!

BR had announced that from 1952 fares by former competitive routes would be charged on a mileage basis. However, in 1951 it was still possible to travel from Euston to Swansea, via Shrewsbury, for the same fare as the shorter journey from Paddington. Dick duly presented himself at Euston and asked for a monthly return to Swansea. The booking clerk laughed – customer care was a long way off then. 'You've come to the wrong station, mate,' he said. Dick quickly disillusioned him and the booking clerk looked at him with new respect as he presented Dick with the ticket. 'You're going to get your money's worth,' he said, to which Dick replied, 'That is the idea!' In fact he never went to Shrewsbury but broke his journey at Wellington to take advantage of the sparse service of the Much Wenlock to Craven Arms line, then about to be closed.

> Dick recalled once being perched on the Princetown branch starter at Yelverton while his companion talked with the porter, who remarked, 'I hope your mate isn't going to be up there for long, my guv'nor's due back in a few minutes and he's a bit militant!'

Dick Riley always liked to position himself above his subject, if possible, from an overbridge, a signal box, or from a signal post, with the permission of the local railwayman if there was one present. Those were free and easy days before the coming of the Health & Safety Executive. This was a standing joke with Ivo Peters, with whom Dick later made many line-side expeditions.

In 1954 Alan Pegler was a director of BR Eastern Region and in September he organised a remarkable special train for fellow members of the Royal Observer Corps from Leeds to Farnborough for the Air Show. Motive power was provided by ex-GNR 4-4-2 No. 251, out of the old York Railway Museum, and ex-GC 'Director' Class 4-4-0 No. 62663 *Prince Albert*. Ivo Peters had driven Oswald Stevens (OS) Nock, the prolific railway author and signal engineer, down to see the train and then went on to Basingstoke shed to record the engines being serviced. It was a glorious September day and there were many photographers present. The story that Ivo Peters used to enjoy telling was this:

> OS Nock: 'Have you ever met Dick Riley?'
> Ivo Peters: 'No, I haven't had that pleasure.'
> OS Nock: 'There he is on top of that lighting mast.'

Thus the two great men met!

Ivo Peters (1915–1989)

Although I never met him, Ivo Peters and I must have often been in the same vicinity on many occasions without knowing it – me as a small boy travelling on the Somerset

& Dorset, and Ivo as the line-side photographer of that same train. It was only many years later that, through Ivo's son, Julian, I became more professionally acquainted with his superb photography of that railway.

Ivo Peters's love of trains dated back to the 1920s when his elder sisters would sometimes take their small brother with them to Saltford station on the GWR main line between Bath and Bristol, to watch the trains. Then, at the age of 10, his mother gave him a camera for his birthday, and shortly afterwards the family all set off for a holiday at Woolacombe in North Devon. Ivo was allowed to travel down from Bath by train, a decision which he suspected his mother regretted slightly for, as a result, he discovered that Mortehoe, the station for Woolacombe, was less than 2 miles from where they were staying – and he spent more time at the station than on the beach. It was at this station that he took his first railway photographs.

From that date until 1934, Ivo pursued his hobby with a vengeance, and as well as taking photographs around his home ground of Bristol and Bath, he was also able to record many parts of the German railway system while holidaying there between 1926 and 1929. It was also about this time that Ivo started his 40-year love affair with the Somerset & Dorset Joint Railway.

In 1934, Ivo went to study at Cambridge, and while there he became hooked on motor racing. Consequently, with all of his spare time devoted to this sport, he had very few railway photographs dating from this period. In fact Ivo did not really take up railway photography again until after the end of World War II. But he soon made up for lost time, and between 1948 and the end of steam on British Railways in 1968, he not only faithfully recorded his beloved S&D and the local GWR railway scene, but also the fast disappearing railways in Ireland, the LSWR main line and branches west of Salisbury, and the 7-mile stretch of the West Coast main line between Grayrigg and Tebay. He also travelled far and wide to photograph the often overlooked industrial railway scene.

LMS 'Jinty' 0-6-0T No. 47557 is snapped by Ivo Peters during a watering stop at Evercreech Junction in 1960

Another 'Slow & Dirty' gem from Ivo Peters. A triple line-up at Bath Green Park in 1952

By the 1960s, with modernisation and rationalisation, the writing was on the wall for steam. The latter half of the decade saw two events which, but a few years earlier, Ivo would have thought utterly impossible. In 1966 his beloved Somerset and Dorset line – the whole 72 miles from Bath to Bournemouth – was abandoned and torn up. And in 1968 the use of steam locomotives by British Railways came to an end. At the time, with the two main props of his railway enthusiasm lost, Ivo wondered whether his life-long love of trains would survive. He was happy to say that it did.

WHAT'S IN A NAME?
Ron White of Colour-Rail found out!

'Jubilee' Class 4-6-0 No. 45651 Shovell, *1959*

In the 1960s few people realised that locomotive nameplates could be bought for modest sums directly from British Railways, and those few people salted away an impressive number of plates. The time eventually came when they had more than they could manage, and surplus ones were then offered for sale (at a suitable mark-up) to the young and innocent. Thus it was that Ron White was approached by one of them and, for £50, was offered a box containing the following items ...

One 'B1' nameplate *Puku*
Two GWR cast iron cabside plates
17 works plates, mainly industrial, some from traction engines

... and so he became, just like that, a COLLECTOR!

> Ron's locomotive nameplates are a very personal collection; not bought as an investment but old friends, lovingly polished on the front (the backs are untouched).

Ron rapidly realized that this boxful was not quite what he wanted in his new status as a collector (apart from the 'B1' plate), and so he decided he had better formulate a PLAN on how to spend what little he had in order to establish his new status; £250 remaining in the sock. The idea he came up with was to purchase one nameplate from each of the Big Four, one British Railways and one Great Central. A total of six plates for £300 – already £50 over his budget.

However, Ron had established a reputation as a restorer of plates (he had access to a stripping and polishing shop) and plates came to him to be lovingly transformed. He was able to convince one customer that he would prefer to be paid in metal rather than cash: Ron would restore his complete collection of nameplates at a rate of £3 a go (irrespective of shape, size or value) if the gentleman would give him one or two of the lesser items which he valued at the equivalent of £66 each (thus restore 22, get one free). So, after restoring 22 nameplates Ron was given *Aston Hall*, and after 44 (this was some collection!) came *Sir Prianius*. That just left an LMS plate to get to complete the Big Four collection. He found out that BR Stoke-on-Trent had an apparently unsellable *Shovell* but he was willing and able to take it. That just left the BR and GCR plates to complete his collection.

By the late 1960s, Mike Higson, of blessed memory, was up and running, first at Hatch End, then at Harrow-on-the-Hill, with a bookshop, also full of nameplates, worksplates … you name it, he had it! Lists were regularly issued, and he had a spring sale with 20 per cent off everything. The smallest Britannia plate, *Ariel*, came down from £75 to £60, less what he owed Ron for cheering up unsellable odds and ends (£2.10), thus the eventual price was £57.10; 42 years later Ron still has it.

That left only the Great Central plate to collect. Mike had just sold the Director Class *Prince Albert* to someone that Ron knew, who happened to be moving house. Ron looked after his collection for many months (no hardship!) and was sold *Prince Albert* for £30 as a thank-you.

The basic collection was in place by 1968, and since then he has quietly exchanged/bought/sold, expanding his treasure trove to 14 plates, plus a load of works plates and South African cabsides arising from too many trips there.

The best bargain? It has got to be exchanging a 'Grange' front number plate (then worth 10 shillings) for a London & North Western Railway nameplate (current value about £10,000). The luckiest deal? Finding the small piece that said FW WEBB'S SYSTEM, which had been cut off when the loco was converted to a *Renown* Simple from an *Alfred the Great* compound – it fitted perfectly. The most amazing? Loading an 'A4' nameplate into an Austin A40 watched by a posse of policemen guarding prisoners at Chesterfield; they were totally uninterested in Ron's struggles. Happy, innocent days.

GAUGING THE WIDTH
The tangled web of railway gauges

It is an interesting fact that today 68 per cent of the world's 661,000 miles of railways are operated using the standard gauge of 4ft 8½in, and this proportion is growing as cross-border intermodal railway operations expand across continents. Apart from the standard gauge, there are several more narrower and wider gauges still in regular use. Of these, the largest in extent is the Russian gauge of 1,520mm (not quite 5ft), which is found across the former Soviet Union countries, the Baltic states and Mongolia; next largest in extent is the 3ft 6in gauge, which is widely used in southern and central Africa, Japan, Taiwan, New Zealand, and in Western Australia and Queensland; the metre gauge is found in many parts of the world including southeast Asia, parts of South America, east Africa and Switzerland; the Indian gauge of 5ft 6in is found in the Indian sub-continent, Argentina and Chile; next is the Irish gauge of 5ft 3in, which is found in Ireland, Victoria and South Australia, and also Brazil; and finally the Iberian gauge of 1,668mm, or just under 5ft 6in, is only found on the Iberian Peninsula.

In Britain, various gauges were used for the early horse-drawn wagonways and plateways, ranging from 4ft 6in for the early 17th-century Wollaton Waggonway and 4ft 1in for the Middleton Railway of 1758, to 4ft 2in for the Surrey Iron Railway of 1803 and 4ft for the Kilmarnock & Troon Railway. In 1804 the world's first successful steam locomotive, built by Richard Trevithick, ran along the 4ft 2in Penydarren plateway in South Wales. All of these gauges had something in common – they roughly measured the same distance as the space between the ruts made by the wheels of horse-drawn carts.

Although the 3ft 6in gauge is found in areas of Japan and Taiwan, recently built high-speed lines in those countries are built to the standard gauge.

Until the 1846 Act of Parliament there were three different gauges being used in Ireland: 4ft 8½in, 5ft 3in and 6ft 2in. After 1846 these were standardised at 5ft 3in.

However, it was George Stephenson, the Father of Railways, who made the biggest impression when he decided upon a gauge of 4ft 8in for his steam-operated colliery railways at Killingworth and Hetton in northeast England. In 1821 George was appointed as Chief Engineer for the Stockton & Darlington Railway, and he opted to use this gauge with another half-inch added to reduce friction on curves – the 4ft 8½in gauge was born and soon became adopted as the standard gauge for the majority of railways around the world.

Despite Stephenson's pioneering work, there were many different rail gauges being used in Britain during the first half of the 19th century, frequently bringing chaos at passenger and goods stations. In 1839 the Eastern Counties Railway opened from Mile End to Romford – built to a gauge of 5ft, it was converted to the Stephenson gauge a year later. The biggest culprit was Isambard Kingdom Brunel, who built the Great Western Railway that opened in 1841 between Paddington and Bristol with a gauge of 7ft ¼in. It eventually took an Act of Parliament in 1846 for the British government to mandate the

standard gauge of 4ft 8½in for new railways in Britain and 5ft 3in for Irish railways, although it took until 1892 before Brunel's broad gauge GWR was completely converted to the standard gauge.

Several hundred broad gauge locomotives await their fate at Swindon Works following the conversion of the GWR to standard gauge in 1892

KING OF THE CASTLES
The story of Charles Collett

Charles Benjamin Collett was born in London in 1871 and, after studying engineering at university, went on to work for marine engineers Maudsley, Sons &

> The company of Maudsley, Sons & Field had been founded in 1798 and specialised in designing and building marine steam engines.

Field in Lambeth. In 1893 Collett moved to Swindon where he worked in the Great Western Railway's drawing office as a draughtsman. He married in 1896 and two years later he was promoted to Assistant to the Chief Draughtsman. Inching his way up the GWR's corporate ladder, he was then promoted to Technical Inspector at the locomotive works in 1900, followed by a swift appointment to Assistant Manager. He held this position until 1912 when he became Works Manager, an important post that he held until 1919 when he became deputy to the GWR's Chief Mechanical Engineer (CME), George Jackson Churchward.

Churchward retired in 1922 leaving an important legacy of locomotive design and construction – standardisation of parts and his four-cylinder 'Star' and two-cylinder 'Saint' Class 4-6-0s were important ingredients that the methodical Collett went on to successfully develop further. Groomed for the job, Collett took over as CME at Swindon and the following year introduced one of his most successful locomotive classes, the four-cylinder 'Castle' Class. Designed

to haul heavy express trains, the 'Castle' was an improvement on Churchward's 'Star' Class, which had been introduced in 1907. So successful was the 'Castle' Class that a total of 171 were newly built or converted from the 'Star' Class over

A luggage label from the world's fastest train, the 'Cheltenham Flyer'

the next 27 years, with some members remaining in service until 1965. 'Castle' Class locomotives became famous in 1932 when they hauled the 'Cheltenham Flyer', then the world's fastest regular express train.

During his tenure as CME at Swindon, Collett introduced no less than 25 new steam locomotive classes, ranging from the humble '1400' Class 0-4-2 tanks, the numerous '5700' 0-6-0 pannier tanks and the powerful '7200' Class 2-8-2 heavy freight tank locos to the 'Hall', 'Grange' and 'Manor' Class 4-6-0s. Without doubt his most famous design was the 'King' Class 4-6-0s, introduced in 1927 to haul the GWR's crack express trains. A further development of the 'Castle', they were the most powerful 4-6-0 locomotives to be built in Britain, weighing 135 tons with a tractive effort of 40,300lb. Only 30 were built and because of their weight were restricted to operating on the main lines from London Paddington to Bristol, Plymouth, Cardiff and Wolverhampton.

The first of the 'King' Class, No. 6000 'King George V', crossed the Atlantic in 1927, only three months after being newly outshopped from Swindon, to appear at the Baltimore & Ohio Railroad's centenary celebrations in 1927.

An able organiser, Collett was also responsible for carrying out a major programme to re-equip Swindon's locomotive workshops, cutting manufacturing costs and improving locomotive manufacturing quality, which itself increased mileages between major overhauls. He also extended the Automatic Train Control fail-safe system over much of the GWR network.

Despite his prolific career as a steam locomotive designer, Collett was amongst the first to see the future of diesel power on railways, and in 1934 successfully introduced the first of 38 streamlined diesel railcars which were widely used not only on branch lines but also as twin-sets with buffet facilities on long distant expresses such as the Birmingham (Snow Hill) to Cardiff route.

Already a widower since 1923, Collett retired in 1941, to be succeeded by Frederick Hawksworth as the last CME at Swindon before nationalisation, and died in 1952 aged 80.

WELSH PHOENIX
The rebirth of the Ffestiniog Railway

Today, the 13½-mile Ffestiniog Railway is a major tourist attraction in the Snowdonia National Park in North Wales, but it hasn't always been so. The rebuilding and reopening of this delightful 1ft 11½in gauge by a dedicated band of volunteers took no less than 28 years to complete.

Back in 1832 the Festiniog Railway Company (then the correct spelling) was authorised by an Act of Parliament to build a railway to transport slate from quarries at Blaenau Ffestiniog to the small harbour at Porthmadog. The railway opened in 1836, but in those early years it was operated by gravity and horsepower – controlled by two brakemen, the loaded wagons of slate would run downhill to Porthmadog, while the empty wagons were hauled back to Blaenau by horses which had travelled down in 'dandy' wagons on each train. The original route included several rope-operated inclines, but these were bypassed by the opening of the Moelwyn Tunnel in 1842.

The horse and gravity operation was a time-consuming and dangerous business, especially if a loaded train grew out of control on the downhill sections. With increasing amounts of slate being produced by the quarries the line had reached capacity by 1860 – steam power seemed the only answer, and in 1863 the first of three diminutive 0-4-0 locomotives were delivered by George England & Co. They were a great success and allowed the introduction of a passenger service in 1865. Four years later the first of the Double Fairlie articulated locomotives was introduced – these double-ended locos could haul much heavier trains and are still a feature of the line today.

With the demand for slate falling, the 1920s brought with it a decline

> The success of the Double Fairlie locomotives on the narrow Ffestiniog Railway led to much interest, and their designer Robert Fairlie staged a series of demonstrations on the line in 1870. These were witnessed by delegations from around the world and led to orders for his innovative locos from Russia, the USA, Mexico, Canada, Australia and New Zealand.

in the railway's fortunes, although a summer tourist service continued until 1939. Slate traffic ceased completely in 1946 and the railway became derelict. Fortunately for us today, a group of preservationists led by Alan Pegler managed to buy the company in 1954 and, after settling its debts, started to gradually reopen the line. The first trains ran a year later across The Cob between Porthmadog and Boston Lodge; Minffordd was reached in 1956, Penrhyn in 1957 and Tan-y-Bwlch in 1958. Here work temporarily stopped as the upper end of the railway was due to be flooded by a new hydro-electric scheme.

A private halt, Campbell's Platform, was opened in 1965 to serve the hostel of Plas Dduallt, and was named after its owner, Colonel Andrew Campbell. He was not only allowed to run his own train down the line to Tan-y-Blwch, but he was also instrumental in the later building of the Dduallt spiral deviation further up the line – being a licensed explosives handler, he did much of the rock blasting on this section.

Undeterred by this setback, the preservationists came up with a cunning plan. Between 1965 and 1978 a 2½-mile diversionary route was built between Ddualltt and Tanygrisiau, taking the new alignment above the flooded section. This deviation includes a unique spiral that gains 35 feet in height for the line and a new 310-yard tunnel. All of this backbreaking work was carried out by volunteers nicknamed 'Deviationists' – many of them highly qualified engineers – in a remote area without road access. The line reopened to Dduallt in 1968, to Tanygrisiau in 1978 and, finally, amid great celebration, to Blaenau Ffestiniog in 1982.

A volunteer hard at work laying track at Campbell's Platform in September 1966

NO MORE BUCKETS AND SPADES
Britain's lost seaside branch lines

It is a sad fact that many seaside branch lines were closed after World War II. Many of the places that they once served owe their existence today to the Victorian railway builders and their backers – for example, on the Yorkshire coast the resorts of Hornsea and Withernsea were insignificant villages until the coming of the railways in the mid-19th century, but both lines fell victim to Dr Beeching's Axe in 1964.

Fortunately a few seaside branch lines that once faced closure were reprieved and are today being used by a growing number of visitors – for example the Looe Valley Line in Cornwall, promoted by the Devon and Cornwall Rail Partnership, has seen passenger numbers nearly double since the beginning of the 21st century.

The southwest of England in particular suffered greatly from the post-Beeching Report cuts. With passenger closure dates given in brackets, the resorts in Cornwall that lost their rail links were Perranporth (1963), Fowey (1965), Padstow (1967) and Bude (1966), while in Devon Kingsbridge (1963), Brixham (1963), Budleigh Salterton (1967), Sidmouth (1967), Instow (1965) and Ilfracombe (1970) all went the same way – although Lynton lost its narrow gauge railway as early as 1935. In Somerset, the long branch line to Watchet and Minehead closed in 1971, but was fortunately revived as the West Somerset Railway, while Burnham-on-Sea closed in 1951.

Back on the south coast, the delightful branch line to Lyme Regis closed in 1965, West Bay (1930) and Swanage (1972), but the latter has in more recent years been reopened as a heritage railway. Closures on the Isle of Wight started in the 1950s: Yarmouth and Freshwater (1953), Bembridge (1953), and Ventnor and Cowes (1966). Back on the mainland, the Hayling Island branch closed in 1963, Selsey (1935), Dungeness (1937), New Romney (1967), Sandgate (1931) and Leysdown on the Isle of Sheppey (1950).

There were also many closures in east England: Aldeburgh (1966), Southwold (1929), Gorleston-on-Sea (1970), Caister-on-Sea (1959), Mundesley-on-Sea (1964), Wells-next-the Sea (1964) and Hunstanton (1969). Up in Lincolnshire, Sutton-on-Sea and Mablethorpe lost their railway in 1970, while further north in Yorkshire both Withernsea and Hornsea lost theirs in 1964. On the Yorkshire coast Robin Hood's Bay station closed in 1965 and Sandsend, Kettleness and Staithes in 1958. In Northumberland the Newbiggin-on-Sea branch closed in 1964, Amble (1930) and Seahouses (1951). Over on the west coast the Silloth branch closed in 1964 and the Wirral coast route through Heswall closed in 1956.

Wales also lost several seaside branch lines: Redwharf Bay (1930), Amlwch (1964), Aberayron (1951), Cardigan (1962), Porthcawl (1965) and Lavernock (1968). Then to Scotland, where on the east coast the Eyemouth branch closed in 1962, Gullane (1932) and the Fife coast route via Elie and Anstruther (1965). St Andrews lost its rail link in 1969, Inverbervie (1951), Cruden Bay (1932), Peterhead (1965), St Combs (1965), Fraserburgh (1965), Macduff (1951), Banff (1964) and the Morayshire coast route via Portsoy and Cullen (1968). Along the coastline of the Moray Firth, Lossiemouth lost its branch in 1964, Burghead and Hopeman (1931) and Fortrose (1951). Further north, the Dornoch branch closed in 1960 while the remote Lybster branch closed as early as 1944. Back down the west coast, the Campbeltown & Machrihanish Light Railway closed in 1932 and the Ayrshire coastal route via Turnberry went in 1942, although the stub to Heads of Ayr stayed open until 1968. Finally this long roll of closures ends in Galloway with the Portpatrick branch closing in 1950 and Kirkudbright in 1965. In memory of happier days.

ALONG THE ROUTE OF THE GREAT CENTRAL
More famous named trains

Until HS1 was completed between Folkestone and London St Pancras in 2007, the last main line to be built in Britain was the Great Central Railway's London Extension between Sheffield and Marylebone.

> Unlike other railways in the country, the Great Central London Extension was built to the Continental loading gauge, as the route was seen as the first step in a railway that linked the north of England with Europe via a Channel Tunnel. The latter project had to wait for nearly 100 years before it saw the light of day.

Serving Sheffield, Nottingham, Loughborough, Leicester, Rugby and London Marylebone, the new railway opened in 1899, offering an alternative for both freight and passengers to the existing Midland Railway and Great Northern Railway routes between London and the North. The GCR became a constituent company of the newly formed London & North Eastern Railway in 1923. Following nationalisation of the railways in 1948, the Great Central route became part of the Eastern Region of British Railways until 1960 when it was transferred to the London Midland Region. Services on the now downgraded route went into decline, with through expresses being withdrawn to leave just a slow stopping train service between the capital and Nottingham. Through freight services ended in 1965, and the end came in 1966 when much of the GC was closed.

The Master Cutler

Between the two world wars there had been a popular restaurant car express that ran on weekdays between Marylebone

> The only named trains that ran on the Great Central route, 'The Master Cutler' and 'The South Yorkshireman' were both introduced after World War II.

and Sheffield. As yet unnamed, it was discontinued during World War II then reintroduced by the LNER in the autumn of 1947 with the name 'The Master Cutler'. The train was usually hauled by 'B1' Class 4-6-0s, but these were replaced in the mid-1950s by former LNER 'A3' 4-6-2s. The morning up train to Marylebone travelled via the direct line through Aylesbury and Amersham, but the evening return service went via the GW/GC Joint Line through High Wycombe and Princes Risborough to avoid commuter traffic. In 1958 the train was rerouted to travel between London King's Cross and Sheffield via the one stop at Retford. Powered by new English Electric Type 4 diesels, the all-Pullman train provided a much faster service for businessmen. The train was discontinued in 1968.

'The Master Cutler' was introduced between London Marylebone and Sheffield in 1947

'The South Yorkshireman' was introduced between London Marylebone and Bradford in 1948

The South Yorkshireman

The second named train to operate along the Great Central route was the weekday only 'The South Yorkshireman', which was introduced by the Eastern Region of BR in 1948. It wasn't exactly an express, as the up service between Bradford (Exchange) and Marylebone via Huddersfield, Sheffield, Nottingham, Loughborough, Leicester, Rugby and Aylesbury took 5 hours 15 minutes. The return down service had the same stops, apart from Rugby which was omitted, and a stop at Penistone which was added, the entire journey taking 5 hours 30 minutes. The train was normally hauled by 'B1' 4-6-0s, although the final one on 2 January 1960 was headed by BR Standard Class 5 4-6-0, No. 73066.

LAND OF PLENTY
A trainspotting trip to South Wales

It was 5 o'clock in the morning on Sunday, 7 April 1963, only 11 days after the publication of the Beeching report that had recommended the wholesale slaughter of Britain's railways. Humming the latest Bobby Vee hit, 'The Night Has a Thousand Eyes', I was standing on the pavement by the A38 in Gloucester – my mission was to visit all the steam sheds in South Wales in one day, thanks to a coach tour organised by the Warwickshire Railway Society. This was probably my last chance before steam in the South Wales' valleys was confined to the dustbin of history and, as it was a Sunday, there was a good chance that most locomotives would be taking their day of rest inside the sheds.

Ex-Cardiff Railway 0-4-0ST No. 1338 at Swansea East Dock in 1963

Ex-Lancashire & Yorkshire Railway 0-4-0ST No. 51218 at Swansea East Dock in 1963

In the pre-dawn darkness, the Society's hired Bedford coach pulled up alongside and my adventure had begun. The other occupants of the steamed-up vehicle just grunted at me as we moved off to our first destination, the Gloucester Horton Road (85B) sub-shed at Lydney where we spotted eight 0-6-0PTs. Next stop was Severn Tunnel Junction (86E) where we arrived at 7am. Here there was an impressive line-up of 66 steam locos. While most of them were freight locos, there were a number of namers: 'Hall' Class Nos. 5932, 5979, 5994, 6941, 6950; 'Modified Hall' Class No. 6977; and 'Grange' Class Nos. 6820, 6873.

Heading off down the A48 we visited Newport Pill (86B) where there were 18 steam of which the majority were the '4200' Class 2-8-0Ts. Ebbw Junction (86A) shed was next, well packed with 71 steam locos including namers locos 'Hall' Nos. 4907, 5939; 'Modified Hall'

No. 6975; 'Grange' No. 6813; and 'Castle' No. 5073. Next was Cardiff East Dock (88L) where there were 44 steam locos including 19 namers: 'Hall' Nos. 4953, 5937, 5942, 6935, 6939, 6957; 'Castle' Nos. 4080, 5014, 5015, 5043, 5051, 5074, 5096; 'Modified Hall' Nos. 6987, 6995; 'Grange' Nos. 6876, 6877; and 'County' Nos. 1000, 1028. Cardiff Cathays (88M) was disappointing, containing only one steam loco, No. 6606, the rest being diesels.

This trip was not for the faint-hearted and as the pace quickened our coach driver dropped us off at Radyr (88B) with 51 steam locos; Barry (88C), 28 steam; Woodham's scrapyard, 32 rusting hulks; Llantrisant (88G), 12 steam;

Tondu (88H), 35 steam; and Duffryn Yard (87B), 60 steam including 'County' No. 1001, 'Hall' Nos. 4919, 6945 and 'Modified Hall' Nos. 6989, 6998. Next on this whistle-stop tour was Neath (87A) which had 58 steam locos including namers 'Hall' Nos. 4910, 4961, 4966, 5981, 'Grange' Nos. 6844, 6845, and 'Castle' No. 7003.

Phew! Now it was up the valleys to Neath (N&B) sub-shed with 11 steam, followed by Glyn Neath sub-shed with five steam then over the mountains to the Rhondda: Treherbert (88F), 11 steam; Ferndale sub-shed, six steam; Aberdare (88J), 45 steam; Merthyr (88D), 14 steam; Dowlais Cae Harris sub-shed, five steam; Rhymney sub-shed, 11 steam; and Aberbeeg (86F), 27 steam locos. By now it was late evening and pitch dark so the driver decided that it was too late to visit Pontypool Road (86G) and in the middle of the day he had also forgotten to visit Aberycnon (88E) – a pity, as I never did manage to visit the latter.

What a day! Worn out, I was dropped off in Gloucester in the late evening with my notebook filled to bursting after visiting 21 sheds and the Barry dump. A total of 619 steam locos were seen although the writing was well and truly on the wall for them and within two years all had been consigned to the scrapyard. R.I.P.

Notebook recording the visit to Severn Tunnel Junction shed on 7 April 1963

INDEX Note: page numbers in bold refer to photographs/illustrations.

0-4-0s 7
0-6-0s 27–8, 47, **123**
2-2-2s **105**
2-4-0s 90, **96**
2-6-2s 28
2-6-4Ts 91
2-8-0s 46
2-8-2s 85
2-10-0s **30**
4-2-2s **73**
4-4-0s 8, 23, 41, 121
4-4-2s 28, **73**, 121
4-6-0s **9**, 30, 38–9, 41, 56–9, **80**, 81, 86, **124**
4-6-2s 36, 39, **39**, 41, **46**, 47, 56–9, **75**, 85–6, **85–6**, 93, 105
4-6-4s 84
'A4's 36, 42, 84–5

accidents 12–14, **13**, 22–3, 62–3, 94
Adams radial tanks 8, 28
Alderney 66, 94
Anglesey 94–5
Appleby Frodingham 66
Ashover Light 20
Aspinall, John 36
atmospheric railways 24–5, **25**
Austen, W.H. 17, 19–20
Avon Valley 66

Bala Lake 79
Basingstoke & Alton Light 90
Battlefield Line 66
Beeching, Richard 52–3, 89
Bere Alston & Calstock 18
Beyer Peacock 50, 78
Big Four 56–7, 70–4, 105, 124–5
Bluebell 66
Bodmin & Wenford 66
Bo'ness & Kinneil 66
Bouch, Sir Thomas 22–3
Bowes 66

Bradshaw, George 88–9
Brecon Mountain 79
Brief Encounter 90–1
Bristol & Exeter 24–5
British Army 17
British Rail 7, 17–18, 20, 30, 39, 48, 52–3, 56–8, 64–5, 74–5, 77, 79, 88–9, 91, 98, 120–5
Brown, Horatio 21
Brownsea Island 95
Brunel, I.K. 24–5, 34–5, 80
Bulleid, O.V. 46–7, 86
Burry Port & Gwendrath Valley 18–19

Caledonian 66
Cambrian 77, 78–9
cargo 110–11, 115–16
Channel Islands 94, 98–9
Chasewater 66
Chesterton, G.K. 87
Chinnor & Princes Risborough 66
Cholsey & Wallingford 66–7
Churchward, G.J. 38, 40–1, 48
Churnet Valley 67
cliff tracks 118–19, **118**
Collett, C. 38, 41, 48, 128–9
Coras Iompair 47
Corris 64–5, 76
Crewe Works 104–5

Dartmoor 67
de la Mare, Walter 29
Dean Forest 67
Dean, William 40–1
diesel-electrics 47–8
diesel-hydraulics 48–9

East Cornwall Mineral 18
East Kent 19, 67
East Lancashire 67
East Somerset 67

Eastgate Station 7–9
Ecclesbourne Valley 67
Edge Hill Light 19
Edward VII 80
Embsay & Bolton Abbey Steam 67
employment 106–7
engine sheds 30–3, **30**, 54–5, 136-8
Epping Ongar 67
Euston-Glasgow express 12–13, **13**

Fay, Sam 45
Ffestiniog 20, **76**, 77–8, 130-1
films 90–1
Flat Holm 95–6
Foxfield Light 67

gauges 34–5, 126-7
  narrow 76–9, 115–17
George V 80–1
George VI 61
Gloucester 7, 9–10, 30, 35
Gloucestershire Warwickshire 67
Gooch, Daniel 35, 109
Great Central 10–11, 44–5, 67, 124–5, 134-5
Great Northern 36, 44, 46, **73**, 92, 113
Great Western 24, 34–5, 38, 40–1, 56–9,
  70–1, 73, 76–7, 79–81, 84, 86, 102–3,
  108–9, 112–13, 122
  Swindon 102–3
Greenly, H. 60
Gresley, N. 36, 42, 46, 84–5
Gwili 67

Hawkshaw, Sir John 108
Hayling Island 96
Holy Island 94–5
Hornby, Frank 92–3
horses 112–13
Howley, Jack 60–1
Hundred of Manhood & Selsey 16
`Hymeks' **10**, 50, **50**

Isle of Bute 95
Isle of Man 96–7, **96**
Isle of Mull 99–100

Isle of Sheppey 97
Isle of Wight 67, 98
Ivatt, H.A. 36, 46

Jersey 98–9
Jones, Haydn 64–5

Keighley & Worth Valley 68
Keith & Dufftown 68
Kent & East Sussex 17–18, 68, 90

Lakeside & Haverthwaite 68
Lartigue, Charles 114–15
Light Railway Act 16–17, 26, 78
Lindisfarne 99
Listowel & Ballybunion 114–15
Liverpool Overhead 82–3, **82–3**
Llanberis Lake 79
Llangollen 68
Lochaber Narrow Gauge 116–17
locomotive exchanges 56–9
London & North Eastern 36, 42, 45–6, 56–7,
  59–61, 70, 72–3, 84–5, 110–11, 113
London & North Western 92, 104–7, 125
London & South Western 26–7, **30**, 98, 123
London, Midland & Scottish 38–9, 42, 57, 59,
  70–2, 73, 84, 85–6, 105, 125
London Underground 7, 72
Lundy Island 99
Lyme Regis 8, 26–8

Mallard 42, 43
Manchester, Sheffield & Lincolnshire 44
Meakin, George 12–13
Metropolitan 44
Mid-Hants Watercress 68
Middleton 68, 126
Midland 7, 44, 92, 113
Midland Railway Centre 68
model railways 8, 92–3
monorail 114–15, **115**

nameplates 124–5
nationalisation 56–7, 70, 74–6, 79
Nene Valley 68

Network Rail 89
Nock, O. S. 121
Nocton Estate Railway 115–16
North British Locomotive Co. 48–9
North Devon & Cornwall Junction Light 20
North Norfolk 68
North Tyneside Steam 68
North Yorkshire Moors 68
Northampton & Lamport 68

Oh! Mr Porter 90
Orkney Islands 100
Owen, Wilfred 101

Paddock Wood & Cranbrook 16
Paignton & Dartmouth Steam 68
Pain, Arthur 26
Peak Rail 69
Peters, Ivo 121, 122–3
Peterson, Edward 16
photography 120–3
Pontypool & Blaenavon 69
potatoes 115–16

Quintinshill 12–13, 14

Railway Children 91
Railways Act 70, 74
Riley, R.C. 120–1
Robinson, John 45
Rolt, L.T.C. 64
Romney, Hythe & Dymchurch 60–1, **60**
Rother Valley 17
royal trains 80–1, **80**
Rye & Camber 17

Sassoon, Siegfried 15
Severn Tunnel 108–9, **108**
Severn Valley 69
Sheerness Line 16
Sheppey Light 16, 18
Shropshire & Montgomeryshire Light 19
Snailbeach District 20
Snowdon Mountain 62–3, **63**
South Devon 25, 40, 69

South Eastern & Chatham 18
Southern Railway 27, 47,
57, 59, 70, 73, 86, 96
Spa Valley 69
speed records 36, 42–3, 84–6
Stanier, W. 38–9, **38**, 85–6, 105
Steep Holm 100
Stephens, H.F. 16–20, 72
Stephenson, G. 34, 127
Stevenson, R.L. 37
Strathspey Steam 69
streamlining 84–6, **85**
Swanage Railway 69
Swansea Vale 69
Swindon & Cricklade 69

Talyllyn 64–5, **65**, 76
Tanfield 69
Tay Bridge 22–3, **23**
timetables 88–9
Tinsley, J. 12–13
Titfield Thunderbolt 91
Transport Acts 52, 74

Vale of Glamorgan 69
Vale of Rheidol 77
Victoria, Queen 22, 80
Volk's Electric 117

war 61, 95–6, 100
`Warships' 48–9, **51**
Watkins, Edward 44, 45
Welsh Highland 20, 78
Welshpool & Llanfair 78–9
West Somerset 69
Western Region 48–51, 75, 120
`Westerns' 50–1, **50**
Weston, Clevedon & Portishead 19
White, Ron 124–5
Wrecker, The 90

Zborowski, Count 60

Amazing and Extraordinary
Facts: The English Countryside
Ruth Binney
ISBN: 978-1-910821-01-5

Amazing and Extraordinary
Facts: London
Stephen Halliday
ISBN: 978-1-910821-02-2

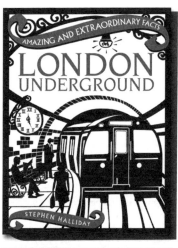

Amazing and Extraordinary
Facts: London Underground
Stephen Halliday
ISBN: 978-1-910821-03-9

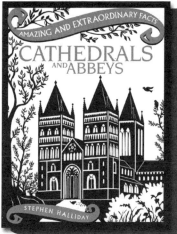

Amazing and Extraordinary
Facts: Cathedrals and Abbeys
Stephen Halliday
ISBN: 978-1-910821-04-6

For more great books visit our website at **www.rydonpublishing.co.uk**

THE AUTHOR

Julian Holland has had a passion for railways since he was a very young lad, and has expressed this as a photographer, author and creative book director. After 35 years following a career in publishing he started to write about his love of railways in 2007 – since then 18 of his books have been published to critical acclaim. Julian travels around Britain giving illustrated lectures, and has also been interviewed on the television and radio on numerous occasions.

ACKNOWLEDGMENTS

Photographs used in this book have come from many sources. Some have been supplied by the photographers and picture libraries credited below. Others have been bought on the open market, sometimes with no information about the original photographer. Wherever possible, photographers or collections have been acknowledged, but some images inevitably remain anonymous, despite attempts at tracing or identifying them. If photographs have been used without due credit or acknowledgment where credit is due, through no fault of our own, apologies are offered.

D. A. Anderson: 80; © David Bailey 2004: 58; British Railways Photographic Section: 34; I. S. Carr: 85; © H. C. Casserley: 26, 30 r; T. G. Flinders: 50 b; C. S. Heaps: 51 r; R. W. Hinton: 39 r; Julian Holland: 11 (both), 30 l, 36, 46, 98, 124, 128, 131, 135 (both), 136 (both), 138; © J. G. Glover: 60; John Goss: 9, 63 (both), 96; N. F. Gurley: 76; Locomotive & General Railway Photographs: 71, 73, 86, 105; John K. Morton: 75; Photograph by Ivo Peters © Julian Peters: 123 both; G. A. Richardson: 51 l; W. S. Sellar: 39 l; Steam Picture Library: 127; J. G. Stevenson: 65.

The poems used in this book have also come from different sources and many were without information regarding the copyright holder. Every effort has been made to trace and identify copyright holders. If poems have been used without due credit or acknowledgment where credit is due, through no fault of our own, apologies are offered.

© Siegfried Sassoon by the kind permission of the Estate of George Sassoon: 15; © Wilfred Owen Estate: 101.